ARE YOU A

"PART-TIME CHRISTIAN"
Or A
"FULLY DEVOTED FOLLOWER OF JESUS CHRIST?"

Why your Answer Could Determine Where you Spend Eternity

Robert and Lisa Laizure

FIVE STAR
PRESS

*ARE YOU A "PART-TIME CHRISTIAN" Or A
"FULLY DEVOTED FOLLOWER OF JESUS CHRIST?"*
by Robert and Lisa Laizure

Printed in China

ISBN 978-1-60477-257-9

Unless otherwise indicated, Bible quotations are taken from the MacArthur Study Bible. Copyright © 2006 by Thomas Nelson,Inc.

www.dollarchristianbooks.com

"Let your heart therefore be wholly devoted to the Lord our God, to walk in His statutes and to keep His commandments, as at this day"

(1 Kings 8:61).

TABLE OF CONTENTS

Chapter 1   Followers of Jesus Must Have Knowledge............17
Chapter 2   Followers of Jesus Help Those in Need.................23
Chapter 3   Followers of Jesus Are Hated by the World..........31
Chapter 4   Followers of Jesus Test What They Hear...............37
Chapter 5   Followers of Jesus Do Not Practice Sin.................47
Chapter 6   Followers of Jesus Show Love 55
Chapter 7   Followers of Jesus Do Not Live Double Lives......65
Chapter 8   Followers of Jesus Will Persevere to the End........71
Chapter 9   Followers of Jesus Know Where They Will
             Spend Eternity..77
Chapter 10   Followers of Jesus Understand Prayer...................83
Chapter 11   Followers of Jesus Have Had A True
             Conversion 89
Chapter 12   Followers of Jesus Live Out Scripture..................93

PREFACE

Yesterday, we turned on the cable network Animal Planet and watched a show called "Growing Up Polar Bear." In it, a baby polar bear was found after his mother and brother had been killed by hunters, and he was taken to a place where he could grow until he was old enough to join other bears in a Canadian sanctuary. He was adorable as he played with toys and barrels, but as he grew older, he started doing something amazing. He took his front paws and jumped onto a blue barrel that was his toy. The narrator explained that he did this by nature because that is what polar bears do to break through the ice! He was in captivity and had never seen another bear do that, yet he did it naturally!

It is amazing, the things polar bears do. They hunt animals, they swim, and they love to eat seals. But what if a polar bear decided he didn't like seals anymore? What if he decided he hated to swim and hated the cold? What if this bear wanted to move to a warmer climate and eat bananas only? What would all the other polar bears think? They might think that he wasn't really a polar bear. Polar bears act like they do because God made them a certain way. They act like polar bears naturally.

The same should be true of Christians: we should act like Christians! When Jesus comes into our lives, He gives us a new nature. As we grow in our relationship with Him, our old ways start to change. Our old ways are replaced by new ways of thinking and acting as we read His Word and obey what it says. We start acting on our new nature. Just like polar bears do certain things because it is in their nature, the same should be true with us as Christians: we have to act on what our new nature demands of us.

This book has **not** been written for those of you who are truly Christians. You truly understand that you are a sinner, saved by the grace of God. You recognize that you still sin, but you have a new nature, one that God has given you, and you are dealing daily with the sin in your life. You are convicted when you sin, you confess when you sin, and you repent of your sin. You understand that you are growing daily; sometimes that means one step forward and two steps back, but you can see a change in your attitudes and actions. Please know this: you are not the target of this book.

This book has been written for those of you who say you are a Christian, but your actions say that you are not. Maybe you lack knowledge, or maybe you have never been told the truth about what it means to be a fully devoted follower of Jesus Christ. You think being a Christian is about a decision you made about Jesus. Maybe you were even baptized, yet you never realized that when you made that decision it had to affect every area of your life. How do you treat your spouse? How do you treat your children? What about the employees you have if you own your own business? What about the people you work with? What do you do with your time and your money? What is the overarching goal in your life? If you attend church or even a Bible Study yet do not adhere to the principles and guidelines taught in the Bible, then we ask you to prayerfully look inward and see if you would fit the status we are terming "part-time Christian."

As we write this, we are in Washington, D.C. As we were riding in a taxi today, we were talking to the taxi driver. He was listening to a radio station, and since the language was foreign to us, we asked him what language it was. He said it was Ethiopian. We were telling him we went to Ethiopia a few years back, and when we asked if he was a Christian, he promptly replied that he was. However, as he was driving, he refused to move out of the way for another car whose driver was very upset with him, and he yelled a few choice words at another driver. Do Christians do things like this as a way of life?

Do Christians have bad days and say the wrong things? Absolutely. Do Christians make mistakes and embarrass the name of Christ? Absolutely. I (Rob) was having one of those days last week.

Not one thing went right at work. My son called and asked a question, and I spent 30 minutes angry with him for something I didn't think he should do. By the time I got home, the younger kids were also home, and I yelled at them because the family room was not picked up. Then I told them I didn't want to be a dad anymore which promptly brought tears to their little eyes. I was getting ready for an important meeting the next day and was waiting for a fax when Lisa came and told me the ink ran out of the fax machine and she didn't have any more in the house. On top of that, our well broke, and we had no water in the house! As we went to bed that night, Lisa said she wasn't sure she wanted to sleep next to me for fear lightening might strike our bed!!

What determines the genuineness of my Christian faith is what I did with my sin that day. I was sickened and saddened by my behavior. I could not be right with my God until I was right with the people whom I hurt that day. I had to apologize to every person whom I hurt. I had to have a repentant, broken heart over what I did. That is true Christianity. That is what a truly devoted follower of Jesus Christ does. We can't just sin and think it is normal. We can't scream, yell, and act rude and disrespectful and just go on with our lives as if nothing in us has ever changed.

Haven't we all heard or said these words?

How could he do that? I THOUGHT HE WAS A
   CHRISTIAN.
How could she say that? I THOUGHT SHE WAS A
   CHRISTIAN.
How could they lie to us? I THOUGHT THEY WERE
   CHRISTIANS.
How could she walk out on our marriage? I THOUGHT
   SHE WAS A CHRISTIAN.
How could he cheat like this in business? I THOUGHT HE
   WAS A CHRISTIAN.
How could he change the deal on us? I THOUGHT HE
   WAS A CHRISTIAN.
How could he have an affair? I THOUGHT HE WAS A
   CHRISTIAN.

How could he swear at his employees like he does?
I THOUGHT HE WAS A CHRISTIAN.

So what is the problem? Why do Christians act like non-Christians? Why do Christians act one way at church and Bible study but act differently at work or at school? Why do Christians profess faith in Christ and still lie to others, cheat on tests, and scream and yell at employees on the jobsite? Why do Christians think people should get divorced if they are "unhappy," accept homosexuality as normal behavior, go to bars, get drunk, and sleep around? What is the problem with this so called "Christian" life?

Aren't we as Christians supposed to be different? Aren't we supposed to treat others differently? Aren't we supposed to be ethical in our business dealings? Aren't we supposed to tell someone we will do something and then do it instead of rationalizing our way out of it? What does being a Christian really mean? Does it affect our lives and the lives of those around us in any way? Why can most people not even tell the difference between Christians and non-Christians?

On vacation this summer, someone told us about a comedy series called "Reba," which we decided to buy and watch. The very first episode gave us a perfect example of the idea of "part-time Christian." In this scene, Reba's husband Brock has just left her for his dental hygienist Barbara Jean. Barbara Jean is pregnant with Brock's child and is living with him. Because of this affair, Reba's life has been turned upside-down: she is now a single mom of three children. None of this would be a problem according to today's world because it happens all the time. The problem with this story is that Barbara Jean claims to be a Christian! Here is an excerpt from a conversation that takes place between Reba and Barbara Jean.

Barbara Jean: "I'm so glad that we can still be friends, I was so afraid that the baby would change the way you feel about me."

Reba (sarcastically): "No, I still feel the same way about you as I always have."

The next scene shows Brock coming in on this conversation as he finds out his daughter, who is a junior in high school, is also pregnant and wants to get married. Here is what is said:

Barbara Jean: "I have to agree with Brock here. Two wrongs don't make a right in the eyes of our Lord."

Reba: "At your church do you sit with the rest of the congregation, or is there a special pew for adulterers?"

Barbara Jean: "Well, actually I sit with the choir."

Unfortunately, as funny as this sounds, this is a tragic scene for truly devoted followers of Jesus Christ. Unfortunately, how Reba feels about Barbara Jean is probably how many unbelievers feel about those who are "part-time Christians." It begs the question: is there such a thing as a "part-time Christian"? Can we spend a couple hours a week doing "spiritual" things yet live the other six days and 22 hours for ourselves? Is this a biblical concept?

First, we have to recognize that we are all born into sin. **Psalm 51:5 says, "Behold, I was brought forth in iniquity, and in sin my mother conceived me."** When we become Christians, we recognize the penalty for our sins has been paid for by Jesus on the cross. **1 Peter 2:24 says, "and He Himself bore our sins in His body on the cross, so that we might die to sin and live to righteousness; for by His wounds you were healed."** Once we recognize we were born in sin and separated from God and we invite Jesus into our lives, the Holy Spirit comes into our lives and starts molding and shaping us to look like Jesus. **Romans 8:29-30 says, "For those whom He foreknew, He also predestined to become conformed to the image of His Son, so that He would be the firstborn among many brethren; and these whom He predestined, He also called; and these whom He called, He also justified; and these whom He justified, He also glorified."** This is a lifetime process. Many things in our lives that displease God He removes quickly, and other things might take years to overcome.

For those of us who have issues with patience, anger, loving others, or kindness, this book is not written to make you think you are not a Christian. This book is written to challenge you to look at your life and see if the sin in your life is being dealt with. Are you less angry than you were last year? Are you more patient with others this year than last? Are you convicted of how you talk to your employees? Are you quick to apologize to those you have offended?

This book is about recognizing what a fully devoted follower of Jesus Christ looks like. That *does not* mean we will ever be sin-free or perfect. It *does* mean that when others see our sin, they will be quick to see our response. Brokenness over our harsh words, apologies over our anger, and true repentance over hurting others will be evident immediately. As we grow in our faith, we will begin to see that others are looking at our lives to see if we are truly living what we say we believe.

A part-time Christian has to make sure, first of all, that he is *truly* a Christian. Nowhere does the Bible say that we live for Jesus on a part-time basis. Our son works as a waiter in a restaurant part-time, which means the rest of the time he is free to do whatever pleases him. As fully devoted followers of Jesus Christ, we have to be full-time believers. We are on the job 24 hours a day, 365 days a year. We don't take time off for vacations; we continue to work for Jesus while on vacations. We don't read our Bibles in the morning and forget what it says by noon. We don't run our businesses or go to work without any thought of how He calls us to act. We don't go through our days lying, cheating, screaming, and yelling when things don't go our way. We don't put God in this little box that we take out on Sunday mornings. That might be what a part-time Christian does, which once again begs the question: Is there such a thing?

The Bible says in **2 Corinthians 5:17, "Therefore if anyone is in Christ, he is a new creature; the old things passed away; behold, new things have come."** A fully devoted follower of Jesus Christ is a new creature; his old life has passed away. The culture we live in says we are allowed to have it both ways. We can have a little Jesus in our lives and a little world in our lives. The culture says we should adhere to the world's standards and embrace divorce, homosexuality, pornography, and adultery. The culture says that, just like

Barbara Jean in "Reba," we are allowed to claim Jesus as our Lord and Savior yet live in a continual pattern of sin. Is that the truth? Is that what being a fully devoted follower of Jesus Christ means?

Please join us as we see what the Bible says about part-time Christianity. Our hope and prayer is that when you are done with this book, you will be challenged to look at your life and determine what it means to be a fully devoted follower of Jesus Christ. Hopefully, you will be motivated to take your faith more seriously and live a life that is pleasing to God. Hopefully, your life will reflect Jesus more, and when others see your life lived out, they will never have a reason to say, "BUT I THOUGHT THEY WERE CHRISTIANS."

Matthew 5:14-16: "You are the light of the world. A city that is set on a hill cannot be hidden. Nor do they light a lamp and put it under a basket, but on a lampstand, and it gives light to all who are in the house. Let your light so shine before men, that they may see your good works and glorify your Father in heaven."

Chapter 1

FOLLOWERS OF JESUS MUST HAVE KNOWLEDGE

Have you ever had a conversation with someone who claims to be a Christian, yet he said things that are clearly not biblical? Have you ever known someone who claims to be a Christian, yet he runs his business without any signs of biblical traits? Have you ever talked to a neighbor or friend who claims to be a Christian, yet the only thing she has to talk about is gossip? What about a conversation with a person who claims to be a Christian but whose advice for an unhappy marriage is divorce? *How can someone who claims to know Jesus give advice that contradicts His Word?*

When Jesus was asked by the religious leaders of His day what the greatest commandment was, we would assume His answer would have been something like, "Feed the poor," "Do good things," or "Be a good person." Instead, His answer was recorded in **Mark 12:28-31: "Then one of the scribes came, and having heard them reasoning together, perceiving that He had answered them well, asked Him, 'Which is the first commandment of all?' Jesus answered him, 'The first of all the commandments is: "Hear, O Israel, the Lord our God, the Lord is one. And you shall love the Lord your God with all your heart, with all your soul, with all your mind, and with all your strength." This is the first commandment. And the second, like it, is this: "You shall love** your neighbor as yourself." There is no other commandment greater than these.'"

How interesting that He said we have to love Him with all of our heart, soul, and mind. The heart and the soul seem to make sense but the mind? What does loving Him with all our minds mean? We would bet that people living in the part-time Christian mode are living that way because they are not using their minds. Being a Christian is not just an emotional experience; the greatest commandment of all tells us that using our minds is of utmost importance. We have to know this God in whom we are putting our trust, and the only way we can do that is to use our minds. Reading His Word is the primary way to come to know Him, and if those who claim to be Christians are not reading their Bibles, how can they truly know Him?

Philippians 1:9: "And this I pray, that your love may abound still more and more in real knowledge and all discernment...."

Colossians 1:10: "So that you will walk in a manner worthy of the Lord, to please Him in all respects, bearing fruit in every good work and increasing in the knowledge of God...."

Ephesians 4:13: "Until we all attain to the unity of the faith, and of the knowledge of the Son of God, to a mature man, to the measure of the stature which belongs to the fullness of Christ."

Somehow, many Christians do not feel the need to read their Bibles; they feel that church on Sunday is all they need in order to learn about God. But they will never love Him with all their minds if they rely solely on what they hear at church. **Romans 12:2** says, **"And do not be conformed to this world, but be transformed by the renewing of your mind, so that you may prove what the will of God is, that which is good and acceptable and perfect."** The Bible is clear that God uses our minds as an avenue for change. As we read and study His Word, we grow in our relationship with Him and recognize our love and need for Him.

We could not imagine our children dating someone whom they only saw one hour a week on Sundays. How would they ever know what this person liked or disliked? How would they know if they could trust this person? How would they ever know what kind of a family this person comes from or what his or her dreams and aspirations are? It would take a lifetime to learn these things if their only interactions were a 40-minute conversation once a week.

The same is true in our Christian lives. In order to be fully devoted followers of Jesus Christ, we must use our minds to get to know Him. We must study His Word on a daily basis so we can see what He asks of us. Consider these issues:

- Pre-marital sex
- Divorce
- Forgiveness
- Dating
- Marriage
- Money
- Children
- Your employment
- Motherhood
- Fatherhood
- Wisdom
- Pornography
- Adultery
- Church discipline
- Possessions
- Patience
- Tithing

Do you know what the Bible says about them? Because we have biblically illiterate Christians and most would rather not take the time to study, we have a world filled with people like Barbara Jean from "Reba." They have no idea that God says adultery is wrong, stealing another woman's husband is wrong, and having a child out of wedlock is wrong. They have no idea that, to truly claim the name of Christ, their lives have to be different than the lives of unbelievers. How is that possible in this day and age? We have Bibles in most every household; we have Christian radio, Christian TV, and

Christian music. We have Bibles on CD, we have sermons on CD, and we have movies of the Bible on DVD. What is the problem?

We don't love God with *all* our minds.

We live in a society where video games, television, and computers take up most of our "mind space." The world we live in demands our time be spent on making more money, moving to bigger homes, and keeping busy with sports or dance. But Jesus says that in order to be fully devoted followers of His, we must use our minds to love *Him* more. That might mean turning the TV off at night and reading our Bibles. That might mean reading a book about marriage or dating. That might mean reading Bible stories to our children before bed. That might mean teaching our children what the Bible says on all the issues listed previously. That might mean listening to sermons in the car on our way to work.

Our church has an outreach ministry to the Spanish people in our area. The problem: we don't speak Spanish. We so desperately want to know this language, but learning it would take time — time which we feel we do not have. But do we really not have the time? We could turn off a few television shows during the week and study Spanish, but we don't feel that motivated.

The same is often true in our Christian lives. We do not feel motivated to learn about God; therefore, we are a generation of biblically illiterate Christians. We do not have the answers for those in need because we refuse to take the time to learn. We run our businesses without the knowledge of biblical wisdom and ethics, and the outside world cannot tell the difference between us and unbelievers.

A fully devoted follower of Jesus Christ is one who opens his Bible and desires to know God. We have to know this God we have put our trust in. We have to learn His ways so we can share Him with others. We have to know the things He loves, like feeding the homeless and taking care of widows and orphans, so that we can do them. We have to know the things He hates, like pride, gossip, and envy, so that we can hate them too. We have to read about Him and His ways so that we can be knowledgeable about how to love Him. It all begins with our minds. Without the time spent getting to know Him, we will be part-time Christians without any impact in this world.

Proverbs 1:7: "The fear of the Lord is the beginning of knowledge, but fools despise wisdom and instruction."

Proverbs 1:22, 29-30: "How long, O naive ones, will you love being simple-minded? And scoffers delight themselves in scoffing and fools hate knowledge? ...Because they hated knowledge and did not choose the fear of the Lord. They would not accept my counsel, they spurned all my reproof."

Proverbs 2:6, 10: "For the Lord gives wisdom; from His mouth come knowledge and understanding...For wisdom will enter your heart and knowledge will be pleasant to your soul."

Proverbs 10:14: "Wise men store up knowledge, but with the mouth of the foolish, ruin is at hand."

Proverbs 11:9: "With his mouth the godless man destroys his neighbor, but through knowledge the righteous will be delivered."

Proverbs 14:7: "Leave the presence of a fool, or you will not discern words of knowledge."

Chapter 2

FOLLOWERS OF JESUS HELPS THOSE IN NEED

1 John 3:17-18: "But whoever has the world's goods, and sees his brother in need and closes his heart against him, how does the love of God abide in him? Little children, let us not love with word or with tongue, but in deed and truth."

Jerry Leastman works as a pastor in Casa Grande, Arizona. For most pastors, that job alone is enough to handle. But Jerry has never been content with that. His overall goal in life is for everyone he meets to come to know Jesus. As a result, Jerry realized that he had to find ways to get out into the community so that others could see the love of Jesus, not just in his words but in his actions as well. He has an incredible heart for the poor and the hurting, so he set up a ministry called "Manna," which serves the poor with grocery carts full of food twice a month. Before people go through the line, they hear testimony of how God saves and changes lives. The food is a way to get people there and to meet their physical needs. Jerry does it with the hope that these people will get fed spiritually.

We asked Jerry about a man named Lalo who became a Christian and now shares the gospel to those who come to their Manna project. Here is what he said:

My first memory of Lalo is of him coming to the church as a meth addict. He had been in and out of prison, lost his family, had no possessions, not a car to drive or even a home to live in. Drugs, sex, and the world had robbed him of everything of value.

I remember going to his place to pick him up for church. It was a small shack with holes right through the walls, broken windows, and no heat or air. Lalo and his nephew were staying there. They had no food, no money, and no water to even wash in. No possessions and no hope.

When Lalo heard the message of God's love and forgiveness, it struck his heart. The realization that God loved and wanted him was a revelation that has changed his life. He now, 5 years later, is studying to go in the ministry and is serving in our church as a director and minister of compassion ministries. His heart is to make a difference to those lost like he was.

Lalo's life will never be the same because Jerry was never content to just talk about his faith; he lived it.

But serving the poor was not enough for Jerry. Jerry is one of these men who never stops. He drives trucks to get the food for Manna, he opened a store where all the income goes directly into his ministry, and he opened a shelter for pregnant women. He is looking to open a car lot so he can get cars for those in need, mainly single mothers who are trying to raise their families on their own. He never stops because he realizes one thing: time is short, and we have to reach as many people for Jesus as we can. He also recognizes what most of us don't: talking about our faith doesn't work half as much as showing our faith by our actions.

In **1 John 3:17-18**, which opens this chapter, John made it clear that if the love of God abides in us, we *will* give to those in need. Isn't that hard for us in America? Don't we look at the less fortunate and say things (though probably not audibly) like, "Why don't you just get a job?" or "Why can't you just quit using drugs? Don't you see how they are ruining your life?" We tend to ignore the fact that maybe they *can't* get a job or *can't* stop using drugs. Maybe they never went to school because their parents lived in poverty. Maybe they don't know how to read. Maybe they were never afforded a childhood that promoted getting an education and working for a living. Maybe they really don't know how. Maybe they lived with parents who were drug addicts or alcoholics. Maybe they cannot imagine a life other than the one they were raised in.

Nicky Cruz was a gang leader on the streets of New York who came to saving faith in Christ and is now an evangelist. You can read his story in a book called *Run, Baby, Run*. In his book *Soul Obsession*, he talks about an outreach that took place in the heart of the Bronx in New York:

> *Even now my mind is fresh with the faces of helplessness I saw in the heart of the Bronx this past summer. Faces of all shapes and colors and ages. Beautiful boys and girls, men and women, blacks, whites, Spanish, Asians. So many were lost. So many needed Jesus.*
>
> *I remember standing on the platform in front of several thousand people packed along the street in front of me. Our stage was set up at the end of a long, narrow street in the heart of one of the most drug-infested neighborhoods in all of New York. High-rise apartment buildings towered over-head on either side. Policemen surrounded the perimeter, watching carefully for any sign of trouble.*
>
> *For several seconds I just stood, surveying the crowd before me. Gang colors were everywhere. Prostitutes and pushers and addicts were scattered throughout the crowd, waiting to hear what I had to say. I glanced at the building surrounding us and noticed people hanging out of their windows, children crowded on fire escapes, teens huddled together on rickety balconies and metal stairways. Mothers and fathers watching through open screens. So many eyes, all looking at me. Waiting. Watching. Wondering.*
>
> *I felt so small and helpless standing in front of them. Once again I knew that nothing I had to say could make a difference. Nothing I could do would erase the pain. It was all up to Jesus. What these people needed was a miracle, and*

only God could provide that. Only God could bring hope to this hopeless corner of the world.

Dear Jesus, I prayed in my heart. Look at them. So many souls. So many poor and hurting people – people who need you. People who are trapped in a sea of poverty and danger and evil. Open their eyes, Lord. Touch their hearts. Use my words to bring them to you![1]

As fully devoted followers of Jesus Christ, we should have the same heart regarding the poor. Just like Nicky said in his prayer, "people who are trapped in a sea of poverty and danger and evil" desperately need help and need to know about Jesus. The problem: it seems a little too dangerous for our comfortable lifestyles. It seems a little too frightening to get involved. Most people in these circumstances were born into poverty and do not have the means to get out. Have you ever wondered why God allows poverty? Perhaps He wants to see how we as His followers will respond. Will we help? Will we allow our world to collide with their world?

Jesus had a heart for the poor, and because He did, we as fully devoted followers should also. Here are some verses that show us His heart:

Matthew 11:5: "The blind receive sight and the lame walk, the lepers are cleansed and the deaf hear, the dead are raised up, and the poor have the gospel preached to them." This is an interesting verse because John the Baptist was in prison, questioning if Jesus was really the Messiah, and Jesus gave him these reasons to prove that He was: the blind see, the lame walk, the lepers are cleansed, the deaf hear, and the poor hear the gospel. Isn't it amazing that Jesus included the poor being preached to as evidence of who He is? That should give us a clue as to how important reaching out to the poor was to Him—and should be to us.

Matthew 26:11: "For you always have the poor with you; but you do not always have Me." Life doesn't seem very fair sometimes. Some people have money and material possessions, and others don't. Why is it that those who are poor have such hard lives? None of it seems fair…until we look at what God has to say about it. We will always have the poor with us. Nothing will ever change that fact. **Proverbs 22:2** says this: **"The rich and the poor have a common bond, the Lord is the maker of them all."** 1 Samuel 2:7 adds, **"The Lord makes poor and rich; He brings low, He also exalts."** Here is what we have to understand: God is the one who has given us our status in life. If we are poor, it is because He placed us there. If we are rich, it is because He placed us there. However unfair that might seem, He is the sovereign God of the Universe who does what He pleases for His own purposes.

If you are a fully devoted follower of Jesus Christ, you understand the heart of Jesus for the poor, and you recognize that God has given you money and has put you in the place where you are for a purpose: so that you can help those less fortunate. We need to constantly pray that God will show us where He wants us. The problem with most of us in America is that we have our own lives and our own mortgages and car payments to be made. We have our secure savings account, and we have our own expenses, so why would we want to give any of that up? We earned it, so why should we give it to those who didn't work for it?

Those are valid questions, ones that we asked Jerry one day. We were wondering about the people who come and get the food at Manna who Jerry knows are just using him. How does he deal with the people who use their food to buy drugs? How does he handle knowing that some people just want to take and take and take without ever coming to faith in Christ? His answer: keep giving them food, and pray that maybe one of these days, the message of Jesus will impact their life. He says everything has to be done with a "hands down" approach which means not wanting anything in return. It is up to God to change their hearts. He only calls us to love them and serve them.

On the other hand, the Bible is very specific in its direction to work hard and be diligent. **Proverbs 19:15** says, **"Laziness casts into a deep sleep, and an idle man will suffer hunger." Proverbs 10:4** adds to that thought: **"Poor is he who works with a negligent hand, but the hand of the diligent makes rich." Proverbs 21:25** adds another thought: **"The desire of the sluggard puts him to death, for his hands refuse to work."**

So, what do we do? Why should we help those who can truly help themselves? **2 Thessalonians 3:10-13** gives us a clue: **"For**

even when we were with you, we used to give you this order: if anyone is not willing to work, then he is not to eat, either. For we hear that some among you are leading an undisciplined life, doing no work at all, but acting like busybodies. Now such persons we command and exhort in the Lord Jesus Christ to work in quiet fashion and eat their own bread. But as for you, brethren, do not grow weary of doing good."

There are people in this world who really don't want to work. Just as 2 Thessalonians says, there are people who lead undisciplined lives. They are unwilling to work (even though they could), and they wander around acting like busybodies. The Bible has a strong rebuke for such people: if you are not willing to work even though you can, you won't be given food to eat. Here is the problem: we don't know the difference. We don't know if someone *can't* work or if he *won't* work. Those who won't are usually mixed in with those who truly need the help. So, do we *not* help 20 because *one* is not doing what he is supposed to? In these instances, we can only pray that the one disobedient person will somehow be touched by the love of Christ and will turn from his ways.

For truly devoted followers of Jesus Christ, helping those in need is not optional. Maybe this help will come in the form of working with the homeless in your area, handing out water bottles in the heat of the summer, or handing out blankets in the winter. But it could also come in the form of helping those in your church. Many single mothers are in desperate need of help. Maybe you could pay for a babysitter for them, buy their groceries for the week, or pay their electric bill. There are so many tangible ways to help others. Maybe you don't have extra money, but you have time on your hands. Maybe you know someone who is sick, and you could mow his lawn or clean his house. Maybe there is a family you know in which the father is out of work; he has put applications everywhere and truly wants to work but cannot find work anywhere. Maybe you could take up a collection at your church to help his family financially while he is in crisis.

Unlike a fully devoted follower of Christ, a part-time Christian does the "church thing" on Sunday, but after that, his life is his own. Why would he want to use his hard earned dollars to help anyone else? Why would he want to help the families of his employees who are struggling financially? What does he care if someone is sick and can't work? Besides, he has his own family, hobbies, and vacations to take care of. According to the way he thinks, everyone should take care of themselves. A part-time Christian lives up to that calling: his only thought is for himself during the week, and he has a few thoughts about God on Sunday.

Remember what **1 John 3:16-17** says: **"We know love by this, that He laid down His life for us; and we ought to lay down our lives for the brethren. But whoever has the world's goods, and sees his brother in need and closes his heart against him, how does the love of God abide in him?"** If we are truly followers of Jesus, we have to care for others. If someone is in need, it is our responsibility to help. Why? To show the love of Christ. We have to recognize that many people have serious problems and could use a little help now and then. For those of you that have a heart to help everyone who crosses your path, make sure you are in constant prayer, asking God to show you whom He would like you to help at that time.

The purpose of helping others and giving to those in need is never to promote anything for yourself. If you have any thoughts like, "Others will think I am so nice," or "I do this just to feel good about myself," then you are helping others for the wrong reasons. Our one and only reason for helping others is to be a sign. If we were traveling and wanted a certain restaurant, we would look for signs pointing us to where we wanted to go. As fully devoted followers of Jesus Christ, we are signs pointing others to Jesus. Never do we want recognition—that is appalling. Never do we want people looking to us—that is frightening. God placed us in the neighborhoods and communities where we are so that we can be a light pointing others out of the darkness and into a relationship with Jesus Christ. That is our purpose in life here on planet earth. Helping others is in the new nature that God gave us the day we put our trust in Him.

Romans 15:26: "For Macedonia and Achaia have been pleased to make a contribution for the poor among the saints in Jerusalem."

Galatians 2:10: "They only asked us to remember the poor — the very thing I also was eager to do."

James 2:5: "Listen, my beloved brethren: did not God choose the poor of this world to be rich in faith and heirs of the kingdom which He promised to those who love Him?"

Chapter 3

FOLLOWERS OF JESUS ARE HATED BY THE WORLD

1 John 3:13: "Do not be surprised, brethren, if the world hates you."

Walking through the streets of Washington, D.C. today, we could hear people yelling. As we got closer, we realized they were street preachers, yelling as loudly as they could, trying to share the gospel with everyone who passed by. Unfortunately, not everyone was as thrilled as we were to see them! Most people listening were annoyed at the inconvenience of having to hear God's Word spoken loudly from the street corner. It is amazing how uncomfortable people got when they were confronted with the truth about salvation. When they heard that Jesus said to "repent," they just kept walking, throwing the tract they were handed into the next garbage can.

I couldn't help but be tremendously proud of the men who were preaching, but on the other hand, I thought their method probably wasn't too effective. I believe God can use anything to bring someone to Himself—even street preachers, if need be. But watching the reactions of the people who passed by was quite revealing. As one lady was walking out of the store, she made the comment, "How sad for those people," referring to the street preachers. How sad? I felt sad for *her*. She could not grasp that she was lost, that she was in desperate need of salvation, and that these men were there to warn her.

I could just imagine how John the Baptist, Paul, or Peter must have felt as they preached, desperate to tell others that hell is a real place and unless they repent and turn to Jesus, they will spend eternity there. But nobody wanted to listen; they wanted to ignore what was being said. Things haven't changed much over the last 2,000 years.

We are all people who want to be liked by others. It would be hard to find someone who truly doesn't care if he is liked or not. Something within us wants the affirmation that people think we are nice or funny or fun to be with. Something within us screams to be wanted and adored. Unfortunately, as a fully devoted follower of Jesus Christ, that isn't always going to happen.

Jesus said this in **John 15:18: "If the world hates you, you know that it has hated Me before it hated you."** In other words, plan on being hated! Paul had the same problem as he was trying to share the gospel: most people didn't like him either! **2 Corinthians 11:25** says, **"Three times I was beaten with rods, once I was stoned, three times I was shipwrecked, a night and a day I have spent in the deep."** Hebrews 11:37-40 adds how difficult it was to be a believer in Paul's day: **"They were stoned, they were sawn in two, they were tempted, they were put to death with the sword; they went about in sheepskins, in goatskins, being destitute, afflicted, ill-treated (men of whom the world was not worthy), wandering in deserts and mountains and caves and holes in the ground."**

Sound a little depressing or frightening, a little like something we really didn't sign up for? Most of us think we wouldn't be very good with the swords or with being sawn in two—sounds a little too painful. But think of the people who are serving Christ in countries where it is illegal to share their faith. Because they continue to do so, they are being put to death. Think of the people who stand on the street corners and beg people to come to Christ yet are scorned and ridiculed. Think of the people who have come to Christ, walked away from a cult or a non-Christian religion, and lost their entire family and all of their friends. Think of the people who have come to faith in Christ and have had to go home to an unbelieving spouse or children.

As fully devoted followers of Jesus Christ, we have to recognize one thing: being hated and misunderstood is normal for us. When we used to live in that "part-time Christian" category, nobody cared that we called ourselves Christians. Our lives didn't really affect others for the cause of Christ, but the minute we became fully devoted followers of Jesus Christ, that all changed. Friends that used to hang out with us don't really want much to do with us anymore. Why?

2 Corinthians 2:15-16 gives the answer: **"For we are a fragrance of Christ to God among those who are being saved and among those who are perishing; to the one an aroma from death to death, to the other an aroma from life to life. And who is adequate for these things?"** When we become a Christian, the Holy Spirit starts changing our lives on the inside. The places we used to go, the things we used to talk about, and even the way we used to talk isn't who we are anymore. If we used to like partying, drinking alcohol, and listening to dirty jokes, suddenly they all make us uncomfortable—not because we are judgmental of others but because God is calling us to holy living now. We can no longer be the people we were before.

That is why people won't like us any more: they don't like who we are becoming. The Bible says that as Christians, we are a fragrant aroma to other Christians. It is fun to be around them, and we have a great time together. But more than that, we share a bond. We are brothers and sisters: we have the same goals in life, and we know where we are going when this life ends. As a result, we enjoy each other's company and want to be around each other. We can share what God is doing in our lives; we can laugh when things are going great and mourn when they aren't. We understand God and His sovereignty; therefore, we think alike. It is like being around someone who has really great perfume or cologne on: we want to be near them so that we can smell the perfume!

However, to non-Christians, we are the aroma of death. They hate what we have become because it makes them feel bad about themselves, so the dinner and movie offers don't seem to come anymore. They hate that we want to tell them about Jesus, they hate that we care deeply where they will spend eternity, and they constantly feel judged (even though they aren't). They do not understand what has happened to us. When our lives reflect more and more of Christ, unbelievers will not want to be around us. As a fully devoted follower of Jesus Christ, you will notice this more and more as you grow in your faith.

As a part-time Christian, you probably won't have any problems in this area. You may show up at church and Bible study, but you talk the same, act the same, and frequent the same places as before. The Christian flag in your personal life has not been raised high enough so that others can see it; therefore, you will not fall into the category of people hated for their faith. At this point, we beg you to "examine yourself to see if you are in the faith."

Fully devoted followers of Jesus Christ will lose friends, family and co-workers because of their stand for Jesus. It happened to Jesus, it happened to the Old Testament prophets, and it happened to Timothy, Paul, and Peter. We can be assured it will happen to us too.

As I saw the street preachers today, I thought about how blessed they truly are because people don't like them! Isn't that a weird thought? But isn't it also like everything else in the Bible that seems so strange to us? Things like **Matthew 20:16: "So the last shall be first, and the first last."** Or **Matthew 5:3: "Blessed are the poor in spirit, for theirs is the kingdom of heaven?"** Everything seems opposite to what the world tells us: we are blessed when we share our faith and people don't like us anymore! We are blessed when people think we are crazy religious fanatics!

Please know this: we are not saying that you should run around trying to get persecuted just for the sake of being persecuted. We are saying that the Bible says we *will* be persecuted for our faith; we won't have to go looking for it! **2 Timothy 3:12** says, **"Indeed, all who desire to live godly in Christ Jesus will be persecuted."**

If you are a new Christian, expecting persecution might seem strange to you, but as you grow in your relationship with Christ, it will make more sense. The more we understand how important salvation is and what is in store eternally for our friends and family who don't know Christ, the higher we will raise our Christian flags. The more we understand God's grace and forgiveness, along with His wrath and anger toward sin, the more we will not care about what others think of us. Our one goal, just like the street preachers we saw today, will be to warn people of the impending danger of not having a relationship with Jesus. Once we truly grasp how important having that relationship is, it won't matter if people like us or not. The only thing that will matter is whether we have shared the gospel with whomever we meet.

Jeremiah had a tough life as a prophet, and nobody ever wanted to listen to him. He kept telling people all the bad things that were going to happen to them, and eventually, he got tired of their lack of response. He experienced the same things we experience as truly devoted followers of Jesus Christ. It can get very frustrating that people won't listen and that they continue living for themselves without any regard to their eternal future. Here is what happened to Jeremiah as he once again brought bad news, this time to Pashhur in **Jeremiah 20:6-8: "And you, Pashhur, and all who live in your house will go into captivity; and you will enter Babylon, and there you will die and there you will be buried, you and all your friends to whom you have falsely prophesied. O Lord, You have deceived me and I was deceived; You have overcome me and prevailed. I have become a laughingstock all day long; everyone mocks me. For each time I speak, I cry aloud; I proclaim violence and destruction, because for me the word of the Lord has resulted in reproach and derision all day long."**

As we try desperately to tell others about Christ, there may often be a similar sense of frustration when nobody listens. Just like Jeremiah, you will want to give up and quit, yet we can be assured that what happened to Jeremiah will happen to us: **Jeremiah 20:9: "But if I say, 'I will not remember Him or speak anymore in His name,' then in my heart it becomes like a burning fire shut up in my bones; and I am weary of holding it in, and I cannot endure it."** Isn't that a great verse? Because Jeremiah loved God with all his heart and loved others more than himself, he *couldn't* stop preaching! As truly devoted followers of Jesus Christ, the same will happen to us. Where we once had a hard time even saying the word "Jesus" out loud, it will become the norm. We may lose a lot of friends and family, but our relationship with the Lord will grow leaps and bounds.

Jeremiah finished his thought with these words: **"For I have heard the whispering of many, 'Terror on every side! Denounce** him; yes, let us denounce him!' All my trusted friends, watching for my fall, say: 'Perhaps he will be deceived, so that we may prevail against him and take our revenge on him.' But the Lord is with me like a dread champion; therefore my persecutors will stumble and not prevail. They will be utterly ashamed, because they have failed, with an everlasting disgrace that will not be forgotten. Yet, O Lord of hosts, You who test the righteous, who see the mind and the heart; let me see Your vengeance on them; for to You I have set forth my cause. Sing to the Lord, praise the Lord! For He has delivered the soul of the needy one from the hand of evildoers."

Remember the words of Jesus in **1 John 3:13: "Do not be surprised, brethren, if the world hates you."** Sharing our faith, living a holy life, and helping others to grow in their faith are not very popular jobs in the world today, yet they have far greater rewards than what the world has to offer—eternal rewards. The more our faith and our love for Jesus grow, the more we won't really care if people like us or not. We will exist for one purpose: living our lives for Him in light of eternity. Just like John the Baptist told his disciples when confronted about Jesus, **"He must increase, but I must decrease" (John 3:30).**

Chapter 4

FOLLOWERS OF JESUS TEST WHAT THEY HEAR

—ɯ—

1 John 4:1: "Beloved, do not believe every spirit, but test the spirits to see whether they are from God, because many false prophets have gone out into the world."

Have you ever wondered how a cult becomes a cult? Have you ever wondered why so many different false religions—even false religions that claim to believe in Jesus—can exist in this world today? Have you ever "tested" your religion against the claims of the Bible to make sure what you are being taught is the truth? Why do people who claim to be Christians seldom do this? What would our world be like today if we as fully devoted followers of Jesus Christ actually picked up books on other religions, read them, studied them, and became knowledgeable enough to have answers for others about why we believe certain things and not others?

How do people get involved in false religions? How could people lose their lives after joining groups like the Heaven's Gate or following false teachers like Jim Jones or David Koresh? What could possibly entice people to follow someone who would brainwash them into thinking that killing themselves for this cause was worthwhile?

The Bible gives us a clear command: test everything to see if it is from God. Unfortunately, instead of testing the claims of false teachers with the Bible as the final authority, people test them with feelings or an overwhelming sense of "God told me." Does God tell people things that contradict His written Word? Absolutely not, but unfortunately, most people do not know that.

Here is the problem: most people do not know God's Word well enough to confront falsehood being taught as truth. That is the difference between a part-time Christian and a fully devoted follower of Jesus Christ. A devoted follower is someone who studies the Bible, is aware of the beliefs of different religions, and has the desire to know the difference so that he can share the truth with others for one purpose: to see them come to know the *real* Christ. A part-time believer is one who doesn't care much for other religions; his attitude is often, "But they seem so sincere," or "If that works for them, I'm sure it is okay," or "I would rather not get involved and cause a problem." As truly devoted followers, everyone should matter to us, which then means that everyone's beliefs should matter to us.

The Bible says in **Galatians 1:6-10, "I am amazed that you are so quickly deserting Him who called you by the grace of Christ, for a different gospel; which is really not another; only there are some who are disturbing you and want to distort the gospel of Christ. But even if we, or an angel from heaven, should preach to you a gospel contrary to what we have preached to you, he is to be accursed! As we have said before, so I say again now, if any man is preaching to you a gospel contrary to what you received, he is to be accursed! For am I now seeking the favor of men, or of God? Or am I striving to please men? If I were still trying to please men, I would not be a bond-servant of Christ."**

We have to understand that there is ONE gospel, and this is it: we were born in sin and separated from God. Jesus, who is God, came to earth as the perfect, sinless Lamb of God and was beaten and crucified for our sins. He was then resurrected, showing us that He conquered death and that He alone is able to take away our sin. As the only way to God, He bridges the gap between us and God that was created by our sin. Salvation is available for those who put their complete trust in *Him* to save them, not a church or a tradition or good works. That is the gospel in a nutshell. Now, take a look at what you believe. See if you adhere to any of these statements:

- There are many ways to God.
- My church is the only way to God.
- I have to be a good person to get to God.
- I have to join a certain religion to get to God.
- There are many gods.
- I can become a god.
- I can work my way to a relationship with God.
- I believe only what my church tells me to believe.

If any one of those statements reflects what you believe, we beg you to search the scriptures alone to see if your beliefs are true. The problem today is that very few people will take the Bible as their final authority; as a result, we have incorrect ideas about who God is and how we can have a relationship with Him. Churches are adding doctrines to the Bible or taking doctrines away from the Bible. Preachers on TV and in pulpits are telling us things that contradict the Bible. Why is it that nobody is standing up and saying, "THAT'S NOT TRUE!"?

We would like to show you how **Galatians 1:6-10** applies to a certain religion: The Church of Jesus Christ of Latter Day Saints or, as we are more familiar with them, the Mormons. Our hope and prayer is that through the words on these pages, we would come to see that if those claiming to be Christians back in the 1800s had adhered to the Bible, especially **Galatians 1:6-10**, the Mormon Church would have never been started.

On the news yesterday, we saw a statement written on the bottom of the screen that said the Mormon Church is the largest growing church in the world with over 12 million members. The next statement said that many evangelical Christian churches say the Mormon Church is a cult. If that is the case, how could something so wrong grow so big? How could something that looks so good on the outside, and which includes good morals and devotion to God and family, be false?

At the lake this year, I met a woman who was waiting for her boat, and we started talking about where she lived. As the conversation went on, I asked her what church she went to, and she told me she was a Mormon. I started asking her questions about her faith:

- Do you know you believe that the God you pray to was a Mormon from another planet who attained "godhood"?
- Do you know that, according to the Mormon church, there are many planets with many gods, and if you are a good Mormon boy who works for your church and does everything right, you could become a god of another planet?
- Do you know that the Jesus you believe in was a spirit child conceived by actual sexual relations between a Heavenly Father (the God you pray to) and Mary?
- Do you know that Jesus and Satan are spirit brothers, according to the Mormon Church?

I was not trying to be a jerk, but I so desperately wanted to show her that what she believes is a "different gospel." Nowhere does the Bible claim there is more than one God. Nowhere does it say that a person can work his way to becoming a god. Nowhere (this borders on blasphemy) does it say that anyone had sexual relations with Mary except her husband Joseph *after* they were married; she was impregnated with Jesus by the Holy Spirit without true physical relations as we know it. Nowhere does it say that Jesus had a spirit brother Lucifer.

In **Galatians 1**, Paul strongly stated, **"But even if we, or an angel from heaven, should preach to you a gospel contrary to what we have preached to you, he is to be accursed! As we have said before, so I say again now, if any man is preaching to you a gospel contrary to what you received, he is to be accursed!"** Has anyone joining the Mormon church ever read this? Has anyone joining the Mormon church ever recognized that an angel Moroni is the one who supposedly brought Joseph Smith this new gospel? Paul clearly warns us that there is *no other gospel*. Anything that someone tries to teach us that is not found in the one true gospel is a false gospel.

We say all of this not to hurt anyone who is a Mormon but to encourage us to study and learn. A part-time Christian doesn't have the desire to "push" his beliefs on anyone else. On the other hand, a fully devoted follower of Jesus Christ has not only a desire but a true passion for the lost, even if that means confronting false religions.

No longer can we just stand here and let others think their false religion is okay. It isn't. More than that, the Bible says that anyone who doesn't place his or her faith in Jesus alone is not truly a Christian and will spend eternity separated from God in hell. Sound a little harsh? Yes, but the truth is that anyone living under a false religion must confront the issue of where he will spend eternity. It is time we learn the true gospel and have the answers for those who need them.

The problem with the Mormon Church is that they say the same words we do, but they do not have the same meaning. They use the words *Jesus*, *Heavenly Father*, *Lucifer*, and *salvation*, but to them, each word has a different meaning than what is in the Bible. Consider the following scriptures as one example:

John 1:1: "In the beginning was the Word, and the Word was with God, and the Word was God."

John 1:14: "And the Word became flesh, and dwelt among us, and we saw His glory, glory as of the only begotten from the Father, full of grace and truth."

Colossians 1:16-18: "For by Him [*Jesus*] all things were created, both in the heavens and on earth, visible and invisible, whether thrones or dominions or rulers or authorities—all things have been created through Him and for Him. He is before all things, and in Him all things hold together. He is also head of the body, the church; and He is the beginning, the firstborn from the dead, so that He Himself will come to have first place in everything" [emphasis ours].

The Mormon Church teaches that God the Father (an exalted man from another planet who achieved godhood over this world) decided on a plan of salvation, which allows those humans who followed it to eternally progress to godhood; therefore, he needed to select one spirit from among all of his spirit children to serve as his chosen leader and redeemer for earth. Two spirits stepped forward to fulfill this purpose—Jesus and Lucifer—and God the Father chose Jesus (his first-born spirit child and the most advanced spirit in the premortal world). God the Father and Jesus then laid out the blueprints for planet earth. Lucifer rebelled and led one-third of the spirits into rebellion, which led to Lucifer becoming Satan and to the spirits that followed him becoming the demons. Brad Melton, a former temple Mormon and missionary who now serves as a Christian speaker and Education Specialist, explained that the Mormon Church teaches that "all humankind and the demons of hell were once spirit brothers and sisters along with Jesus and Lucifer; Jesus was begotten by physical relations between God the Father and his spirit daughter Mary and this unique parentage on earth sets Jesus apart from the rest of us."[2]

Does that sound like the same God or Jesus described in the scriptures above??

The Bible clearly states that by Jesus, *all* things were created which also means that He created angels and demons. He created Lucifer—Lucifer was not His brother. He was *not* a spirit baby somewhere who attained godhood by being a good Mormon. The Bible says in **2 Timothy 3:16-17, "All scripture is inspired by God and profitable for teaching, for reproof, for correction, for training in righteousness; so that the man of God may be adequate, equipped for every good work."** The Word of God *alone* is where we find all of our answers, but unfortunately, many religions are adding doctrines, traditions, rules, and regulations to the Bible. We as fully devoted followers of Jesus Christ do not have that option; God's Word alone is the only inspired scripture for which He takes credit. The Word of God *must* be the final authority in our lives; nothing should ever be added or taken away from what it says.

We beg you read your Bible and learn what true, biblical Christianity is all about. We beg you to read books in order to learn about false religions. We beg you to sign up for classes that people like Brad Melton teach, classes that will help you understand the differences between biblical beliefs and cults. We are shocked when we hear that false religions are growing numerically, yet their growth makes sense because a lack of knowledge of the truth has infiltrated our churches and our lives. As fully devoted followers of Jesus Christ, we have to know what we believe and take a stand for it. We live in a world that expects us to go along with everyone, not make a scene, never question someone's belief in God, and never confront someone for his "personal religion." That kind of blanket acceptance of every belief is not an option for someone who is a fully devoted follower of Jesus Christ.

Did Jesus confront false religion? Take a look at what He told the Pharisees, a very religious sect who felt that doing good works was the way to God. Jesus did *not* just tolerate their religion and act as if their false beliefs were okay. He refused to think, "I'm okay, you're okay," and He refused to keep silent. The same should be true of us if we claim to be fully devoted followers of Jesus Christ.

Matthew 23:13-15: "But woe to you, scribes and Pharisees, hypocrites, because you shut off the kingdom of heaven from people; for you do not enter in yourselves, nor do you allow those who are entering to go in. Woe to you, scribes and Pharisees, hypocrites, because you devour widows' houses, and for a pretense you make long prayers; therefore you will receive greater condemnation. Woe to you, scribes and Pharisees, hypocrites, because you travel around on sea and land to make one proselyte; and when he becomes one, you make him twice as much a son of hell as yourselves."

He went on to say in **Matthew 23:23-30, "Woe to you, scribes and Pharisees, hypocrites! For you tithe mint and dill and cummin, and have neglected the weightier provisions of the law: justice and mercy and faithfulness; but these are the things you should have done without neglecting the others. You blind guides, who strain out a gnat and swallow a camel! Woe to you, scribes and Pharisees, hypocrites! For you clean the outside of the cup and of the dish, but inside they are full of robbery and self-indulgence. You blind Pharisee, first clean the inside of the cup and of the dish, so that the outside of it may become clean also. Woe to you, scribes and Pharisees, hypocrites! For you are like whitewashed tombs which on the outside appear beautiful, but inside they are full of dead men's bones and all uncleanness. So you, too, outwardly appear righteous to men, but inwardly you are full of hypocrisy and lawlessness. Woe to you, scribes and Pharisees, hypocrites! For you build the tombs of the prophets**

and adorn the monuments of the righteous, and say, 'If we had been living in the days of our fathers, we would not have been partners with them in shedding the blood of the prophets.'"

If Jesus was outraged at false religion, why wouldn't we be? Why do we *not* care that our friends and relatives are consumed by false teaching? Why do we *not* study and learn everything we can so that we can have true, biblical answers for them? The Bible has serious issues with false teachers, and God made sure we could recognize them when we see them. However, because we have a nation of people who do not read their Bibles, masses of people join cults. Here is what the Bible has to say about such false teachers:

2 Peter 2:1: "But false prophets also arose among the people, just as there will also be false teachers among you, who will secretly introduce destructive heresies, even denying the Master who bought them, bringing swift destruction upon themselves."

Plan on destructive heresies being introduced into the churches, and plan on false teachers bringing false messages. *The Bible makes it clear that we are to be cautious.*

2 Corinthians 11:13: "For such men are false apostles, deceitful workers, disguising themselves as apostles of Christ."

Paul says in this verse that false teachers disguise themselves as apostles of Christ. Don't we so often say things like, "But they say they are Christians," or "He preaches from the Bible"? We have to be on the alert for false teachers who seem genuine. If they preach a different gospel, they are false.

Revelation 2:22: "I know your deeds and your toil and perseverance, and that you cannot tolerate evil men, and you put to the test those who call themselves apostles, and they are not, and you found them to be false."

This church in Revelation is a model for us in testing those who call themselves apostles. If you are being told that you have to do certain things for your church, wear certain clothes, repeat a certain prayer over and over to be forgiven, or hand over all your money, please compare what you are being told with what the Bible says. *Never* take a pastor's word for something without comparing what he says with what the Bible says. If you are uncomfortable with or even have a question about something being taught, go to a Christian bookstore, and find sound biblical commentaries to study what you are being taught. We have to take seriously the idea that false teachers and false prophets will infiltrate the churches.

Matthew 7:15: "Beware of the false prophets, who come to you in sheep's clothing, but inwardly are ravenous wolves."

Jesus wanted to make it perfectly clear that false prophets look like innocent lambs or sheep. They say the right things, have charismatic personalities, and win over many people to their false religion because they appear harmless. Jesus said they are wolves underneath their harmless façade, and He wanted to make sure we would know to look deep within the teachings of such people.

Matthew 24:11: "Many false prophets will arise and will mislead many."

This verse is so sad to us because it says that many people will be misled into false religions because they will not know any better. This brings us back to our central question: why would they be so easily misled? Without a clear understanding of the Bible, the knowledge of who God and Jesus are, and the ability to recognize false teaching, they wouldn't know any better. Without the basics of God's Word, we too could be misled into false teaching.

Matthew 24:24: "For false Christs and false prophets will arise and will show great signs and wonders, so as to mislead, if possible, even the elect."

Here is a scary thought: these false prophets will show us great signs and wonders. Maybe it will be a great miracle like rain in the midst of a drought, or maybe someone will be healed of cancer. Whatever these signs and wonders are, people who claim to be Christians could possibly be misled. Are we beginning to see how urgent it is for us to know God's Word inside and out? We *have* to know what to expect in the future, and we *have* to know what the truth is so we can recognize false teaching when we hear it. Those abilities will only come about as we take seriously the study of our Bibles.

So, here is the point: part-time Christians have little desire to study and learn about cults and false religions. They have little desire to confront others with the truth, and they refuse to get involved with God's call on their lives. However, Jesus said that our job is doing just that:

Matthew 28:19-20: "Go therefore and make disciples of all the nations, baptizing them in the name of the Father and the Son and the Holy Spirit, teaching them to observe all that I commanded you; and lo, I am with you always, even to the end of the age."

On the other hand, a fully devoted follower of Jesus Christ recognizes that he is saved for this purpose: to go and make disciples. He is a Christian so that he can teach others all that Jesus has commanded. He desperately wants to know the true gospel so that he can share it with others. He will do exactly what **1 John 4:1** says: **"Beloved, do not believe every spirit, but test the spirits to see whether they are from God, because many false prophets have gone out into the world."**

Which begs the question once again…

Is there such a thing, according to the Bible, as a part-time Christian?

Chapter 5

FOLLOWERS OF JESUS DO NOT PRACTICE SIN

1 John 3:9: "No one who is born of God practices sin, because His seed abides in Him; and he cannot sin, because he is born of God."

1 John is a difficult book in the Bible because it deals so much with our actions as Christians. It demands that we understand what being a truly devoted follower of Jesus Christ really means. When we refer to sin in this chapter, we are not talking about the sin that God is dealing with in the lives of devoted Christians. We are talking about people who live in a continually unrepentant lifestyle of sin over a long period of time, without any thought or conviction to change, but who continue to claim to be Christians. The first question that comes to most people after reading this last statement is, "What is considered a long period of time?" The real question ought to be, "Are you practicing sin?" If so, we challenge you to look at your life and see if your part-time Christian status even means you are a Christian at all.

1 John 3:4-10: "Everyone who practices sin also practices lawlessness; and sin is lawlessness. You know that He appeared in order to take away sins; and in Him there is no sin. No one who abides in Him sins; no one who sins has seen Him or knows Him. Little

children, make sure no one deceives you; the one who practices righteousness is righteous, just as He is righteous; the one who practices sin is of the devil; for the devil has sinned from the beginning. The Son of God appeared for this purpose, to destroy the works of the devil. No one who is born of God practices sin, because His seed abides in him; and he cannot sin, because he is born of God. By this the children of God and the children of the devil are obvious: anyone who does not practice righteousness is not of God, nor the one who does not love his brother."

When we become Christians, the Holy Spirit takes up residence in our lives and begins to change us from the inside. The seed of God is placed in us, and as a result, we cannot live a continual life of sin. The Bible tells us that that if we are not continually practicing righteousness, then we truly aren't His. Take a look at these scenarios, and see which one best fits your life.

IF YOU ARE SINGLE

You go to church on Sundays and show up at a Bible study group but on the weekends, you go out to clubs, drinking and looking for someone to have sex with. You know what the Bible says about promiscuity and drinking, but you are lonely and decide the Bible is a little old fashioned for this day and age.

Would you be considered a part-time Christian?

You go to church on Sundays, attend a Bible study group and yet you refuse to go to clubs on the weekend for the purpose of drinking and sex. You recognize that you are to be light in a dark, unbelieving world. You have given your life to Jesus, and you will wait for the mate He has for you, which means waiting for someone who is a truly devoted follower of Jesus Christ. Even when loneliness takes over, you refuse to compromise your standards, knowing that God will bless you in His time.

Would you be considered a fully devoted follower of Jesus Christ?

IF YOU OWN YOUR OWN BUSINESS

You go to church on Sundays and show up at a Bible Study in the middle of the week but you tend to not treat the people who work for you the way the Bible calls you to. You yell at your employees, you swear at them during the day, you are unkind to them, you refuse to pay them on time, and you have no interest in their spiritual well being.

Would you be considered a part-time Christian?

You go to church on Sundays and attend a Bible Study in the middle of the week but because you own your own business, you recognize the blessing and responsibility God has given you. You are called to be a light to your employees and the people you do business with. You are called to share your faith with those you come in contact with. You are to love them regardless of their race or religion. You take this job very seriously because it has been given to you by God.

Would you be considered a fully devoted follower of Jesus Christ?

IF YOU ARE A HUSBAND

You go to church on Sundays and show up at a Bible Study in the middle of the week, but during the week, you are unkind, demand sex regardless of your wife's feelings, are disrespectful, and refuse to care more for her than yourself. You flirt with others at the office, work beyond what you have to without regard to your wife, and would rather be out with your friends than at home building your family up.

Would you be considered a part-time Christian?

You go to church and attend a Bible Study in the middle of the week but during the week, you understand your role as a husband as described in **Ephesians 5:25**: **"Husbands, love your wives, just**

as Christ also loved the church and gave Himself up for her." Because of your love for Christ, you care more for your wife than you do yourself. You respect her, love her, provide for her, and give yourself completely to her alone.

Would you be considered a fully devoted follower of Jesus Christ?

IF YOU ARE A WIFE

You go to church and show up at a Bible Study in the middle of the week and yet during the week, you refuse to respect your husband, refuse to come under his authority as the leader of the home, gossip about him to others, and refuse to have sex with him.

Would you be considered a part-time Christian?

You go to church and attend a Bible Study in the middle of the week and yet during the week, you obey what **Ephesians 5:22** says: **"Wives, be subject to your own husbands, as to the Lord."** You respect your husband as a gift from God; you recognize his need for sex and refuse to withhold it from him. You encourage him, love him, stand by him, and refuse to talk negatively about him to others.

Would you be considered a fully devoted follower of Jesus Christ?

Through this little scenario exercise, we want you see one thing: both part-time Christians and fully devoted followers of Jesus Christ go to church and attend Bible Study. That is our point: just because you go to church and Bible study, does that automatically mean you are a Christian? A fully devoted follower of Jesus Christ lives out his faith during the week in all situations of life. At work, he trusts God, looking for ways to share his faith and is a faithful employee or employer. In marriage or singleness, he lives out what he is being taught in church or Bible Study.

If you are not practicing righteousness on a daily basis, can you be a Christian as **1 John 3:4-10** defines one? If you are living in a continually unrepentant lifestyle at work or at home, without regard to how God calls you to live, can you be a Christian as the Bible defines one? Remember, this book was written as a check-up for ourselves. The Bible says that, as fully devoted followers of Jesus Christ, we *cannot* live two different lifestyles. We cannot do the "Christian thing" on Sundays and then live a completely different lifestyle during the week. It is time for people to know that the Bible, which is the final authority in our lives, says it is impossible to be a truly devoted follower of Jesus Christ and live two separate lives.

We hear stories all the time from husbands who are frustrated with their wives. They go to Bible studies during the week and go to church on the weekends, yet they refuse to live out what they are taught when they get home. They are disrespectful, refuse to honor their husbands and their authority, and continually demean their husbands in front of others, including their children.

We also hear stories all the time from wives who are frustrated with their husbands who go to church and Bible Study during the week yet refuse to be the spiritual leaders of their homes. These men refuse to honor their wives, look at other women, look at pornography, and refuse to live out what they are taught at church. What is the problem?

Part-time Christianity is the problem: our churches need to be preaching the truth on this subject. However, many fear that if these truths were taught from the pulpit, many people would leave. But these truths *have* to be taught. People *have* to know that the Bible does not recognize the idea of part-time Christianity. Men who claim to be Christians need to recognize what that means in their workplace and their home life. Women who claim to be Christians need to recognize that Christianity is not a part-time job; it means a change in life at home and with our families. We cannot pick and choose what we want to believe and how we want to live.

We love the church we go to because the number of people in attendance has never been the driving force. Money is not talked about unless it happens to be in the scriptures, and the offering plate is never passed. If you want to give, you put the money in a box in the back. Because the church is not driven by money, our pastor has no problem just preaching the truth of scripture. He is not worried that people might leave if he offends them. In fact, he recognizes that the Bible is often offensive! Anyone living in sin doesn't want to come to church to hear about it, yet the Bible says without any regrets in **2 Timothy 4:2-3, "Preach the word; be ready in season and out of season; reprove, rebuke, exhort, with great patience and instruction. For the time will come when they will not endure sound doctrine; but wanting to have their ears tickled, they will accumulate for themselves teachers in accordance to their own desires,..."**

The point is that the number of people attending our churches shouldn't mean anything. However, making sure that the people who *are* coming to church are fully devoted followers of Jesus Christ should mean everything. The Bible says the "road is very narrow and very few will find it," so it would make sense that if God's Word is truly being taught, sin is being dealt with, and holy living is being promoted, churches might not be as big as some would like.

It would be interesting to ask your pastor this question: "Would you rather have 500 fully devoted followers of Jesus Christ or 3,000 part-time Christians?" The 3,000 part-time Christians might bring a lot more money into a church, but the 500 fully devoted followers of Jesus Christ will have a bigger impact on this world for His Kingdom.

We need our churches to get back to preaching the truth about what it means to be a true believer in Christ. We need our churches to quit promoting a false version of Christianity. We need our churches to wake up and talk about sin, repentance, humility, and holiness. We need our churches to stop preaching sermons that will make us walk out feeling happy about ourselves; instead, we need sermons that challenge us to live obedient, godly lives.

We need our churches to teach men how to be the spiritual leaders of their homes. We need our churches to teach women how to love and respect their husbands. We need our churches to teach our children that they are not Christians because their parents are but that they have to come to saving faith in Christ themselves. We need pastors to start preaching the truth about what it takes to be fully devoted followers of Jesus Christ.

True Christianity will have an enormous impact on this world if we understand that our lives are meant to be lived differently than the lives of unbelievers. We cannot live in a continual pattern of sin without any conviction to change. We are always amazed to see people who go to church and claim the name of Christ yet live together unmarried. Do these people have any idea what their behavior does to the cause of Christ? Do people have any idea how it hurts their witness and their reputation as Christians? Their impact for Jesus has just been made void.

You can insert any continual pattern of sin in the place of living together before marriage: adultery, drunkeness, bad language, unkindness, pride, greed, materialism, and so on. Anything that forms a *continually unrepentant* pattern of living that disobeys God's Word destroys our reputations as Christians. Why would anyone listen to us?

In **Revelation 2:5,** Jesus told the church at Ephesus, **"Therefore remember from where you have fallen, and repent and do the deeds you did at first; or else I am coming to you and will remove your lampstand out of its place—unless you repent."** If this church did not repent, Jesus would take away their light and their impact in the world. What a frightening thought: they would say they were Christians, but because of their actions, no one would take them seriously. Why would others come to Jesus when they are being preached to by hypocrites?

Truly devoted followers of Jesus Christ understand that living continually unrepentant lifestyles is not an option. Part-time Christians, on the other hand, do not understand, or have never been taught, that the Bible says it is not possible to live this way. 1 John makes it very clear that, as Christians, we have been born of God; His seed lives in us. As a result, we will be convicted of lifestyles, attitudes, and actions that contradict His life in us, and our hearts will be moved to repent and turn away from those lifestyles, attitudes, and actions.

Please check your own life. Can *you* tell that God lives in you? Can *others* see that God lives in you? If not, we beg you to confront the sin in your life, confess it as sin, and walk away from it. That is what a truly devoted follower of Jesus Christ *must* do!

Chapter 6

FOLLOWERS OF JESUS
SHOW LOVE

1 John 2:3-7: "By this we know that we have come to know Him, if we keep His commandments. The one who says, 'I have come to know Him,' and does not keep His commandments, is a liar, and the truth is not in him; but whoever keeps His word, in him the love of God has truly been perfected. By this we know that we are in Him: the one who says he abides in Him ought himself to walk in the same manner as He walked. Beloved, I am not writing a new commandment to you, but an old commandment which you have had from the beginning; the old commandment is the word which you have heard."

The Bible says that we will know if we truly belong to Christ if we "keep His commandments." That sounds frightening and impossible, yet 1 John identifies obedience as the true test of our faith. If we do not keep His commandments, then the Bible says we are liars. **John 15:14** says the same thing: **"You are My friends if you do what I command you." John 15:10** also adds, **"If you keep My commandments, you will abide in My love; just as I have kept My Father's commandments and abide in His love."**

If keeping the commands of Jesus is a true test of a fully devoted follower of Jesus Christ, then we need to look at what His commands are. We started wondering about what Jesus commanded us to do, and in Matthew we found things like "Do not murder," and "Do not commit adultery." We also found things like "Give to him who asks of you," "Do not store up treasures for yourselves," and "Forgive others." What we realized is that all of these things fit under what Jesus called the two greatest commandments which are found in **Mark 12:28-31: "One of the scribes came and heard them arguing, and recognizing that He had answered them well, asked Him, 'What commandment is the foremost of all?' Jesus answered, 'The foremost is, "Hear, O Israel! The Lord our God is one Lord; and you shall love the Lord your God with all your heart, and with all your soul, and with all your mind, and with all your strength." The second is this, "You shall love your neighbor as yourself." There is no other commandment greater than these.'"**

The commandments of Jesus center on two things that should permeate our lives: first, loving God with all our heart, soul, mind and strength and, second, loving our neighbor as ourselves. As fully devoted followers of Jesus Christ, everything in our lives should center on these two commandments. Now, let's take a look back into the Old Testament, see what the original Ten Commandments are, and see if they relate to what Jesus had to say.

❖ Commandment 1: **Exodus 20:3: "You shall have no other gods before Me."**

In order to be a fully devoted follower of Jesus Christ, we can have *no* other gods before Him. Nothing in our lives should be more important than God and His mission for us, not even the things on this list:

- Job
- Children
- Spouse
- Girlfriend or boyfriend
- Sports
- Hobby
- Money

- House
- Car
- Vacation home
- Ambitions
- Status
- Power
- Time
- Church
- Bible study
- Ministry

A part-time Christian is one who places any of these things before God Himself. A part-time Christian does not realize that all of these things are gifts *from* Him to be used *for* Him. He wants our total devotion to be to *Him*; nothing should be more important in our lives. God has given you your job in order for you to share Him with others. He has given you your money, ambitions, and status so that He can use you to share Him with others. He has given you your spouse and your children so you can teach them about a relationship with Christ. He has given you each day you are alive to be used by Him. Nothing should come before His call on your life.

This first of the Ten Commandments is similar to the words of Jesus: "Love the Lord your God with all your heart, soul, mind and with all your strength."

❖ Commandment 2: **Exodus 20:4-6: "You shall not make for yourself an idol, or any likeness of what is in heaven above or on the earth beneath or in the water under the earth. You shall not worship them or serve them; for I, the Lord your God, am a jealous God, visiting the iniquity of the fathers on the children, on the third and the fourth generations of those who hate Me, but showing lovingkindness to thousands, to those who love Me and keep My commandments."**

God is very serious about our devotion to Him and not an object. In the Old Testament, people felt the need to worship something they could touch and feel, but God wants us to worship Him by faith. **Deuteronomy 4:15-19** says, **"You saw no form of any kind the day the Lord spoke to you at Horeb out of the fire. Therefore watch yourselves very carefully, so that you do not become corrupt and make for yourselves an idol, an image of any shape, whether formed like a man or a woman, or like any animal on earth or any bird that flies in the air, or like any creature that moves along the ground or any fish in the waters below. And when you look up to the sky and see the sun, the moon and the stars—all the heavenly array—do not be enticed into bowing down to them and worshiping things the Lord your God has apportioned to all the nations under heaven."**

A few years ago we went to Italy and were amazed at the magnificent churches we saw. We were even more amazed at the statues and objects that people bowed and prayed to. The Bible is very clear on this subject: God wants none of this for His followers. When Jesus met the woman at the well in **John 4:23-24,** He made it clear to her that there was no certain building or place in which people needed to worship. He wanted her to know that we worship Him in spirit and truth. He does not want us looking at an object or the stars and bowing down to them. He wants our hearts to be totally devoted to Him: **"Yet a time is coming and has now come when the true worshipers will worship the Father in spirit and truth, for they are the kind of worshipers the Father seeks. God is spirit, and his worshipers must worship in spirit and in truth."**

This second of the Ten Commandments is similar to the words of Jesus: "Love the Lord your God with all your heart, soul, mind and all your strength."

❖ Commandment 3: **Exodus 20:7: "You shall not misuse the name of the Lord your God, for the Lord will not hold anyone guiltless who misuses his name."**

God is holy, and His name is to be revered. However, in the culture in which we live, using His name in vain is normal. How many times do we hear people say, "I swear to God"? How many television shows throw around the name "God" as just a normal word? We are so used to it that we are not fazed in the least when we hear it. But God is serious about us as His children using His name reverently.

This third of the Ten Commandments is similar to the words of Jesus: "Love the Lord your God with all your heart, soul, mind and all your strength."

❖ Commandment 4: **Exodus 20:8-11: "Remember the Sabbath day by keeping it holy. Six days you shall labor and do all your work, but the seventh day is a Sabbath to the Lord your God. On it you shall not do any work, neither you, nor your son or daughter, nor your manservant or maidservant, nor your animals, nor the alien within your gates. For in six days the Lord made the heavens and the earth, the sea, and all that is in them, but he rested on the seventh day. Therefore the Lord blessed the Sabbath day and made it holy."**

How many people do we know who work all the time? They could not possibly take a day off because they have so much to do. But God had a different plan: remember the Sabbath, and keep it holy.

In the past, we had always gone to large churches where we could slip in and out of easily without ever being noticed. However, our current church was small enough when we first started attending that we had to get to know people! We had never done that before! Through that process, we learned is how truly important these people are in our lives. We worship together, serve together, and learn together. But what if we never went to church on Sunday? What if we never took the time to get involved? The Sabbath day is so important to God that He claimed it for Himself, and as believers we should recognize its importance. He made this day for Himself. Once again, it has to all be about Him.

This fourth of the Ten Commandments is similar to the command of Jesus: "Love the Lord your God with all your heart, soul, mind and with all your strength."

> ❖ Commandment 5: **Exodus 20:12: "Honor your father and your mother, so that you may live long in the land the Lord your God is giving you."**

The first four Old Testament commandments deal with how important God is, how we should speak of Him, and how our lives are to be used for Him. Now, we turn to the second of Jesus' commandments: "Love your neighbor as yourself." Of the Ten Commandments, numbers 5-10 all comment on how we should treat other people. Commandment 5 teaches us how important it is to honor our parents.

For some of you, honoring your parents is difficult because you were raised in a home where your parents hurt you more than loved you. Yet God calls you to honor them regardless. It can be so hard to do what God asks of us when we have been hurt. Jesus' commandment to love others is one that many of us would like to delete out of our Bibles, but since we can't, we have to treat others who have hurt us with the kind of love described in **1 Corinthians 13**:

Patient, kind, not jealous, does not brag, is not arrogant, does not act unbecomingly, does not seek my own, is not provoked, does not take into account a wrong suffered, does not rejoice in unrighteousness, rejoices with the truth, bears all things, believes all things, hopes all things and endures all things.

We'd like to share a situation with you has nothing to do with honoring your father and mother, but it does relate to loving others regardless of what they do to you. A while back, someone hurt Rob in a business deal, and I (Lisa) cried for days; I was so upset that the wrong done against Rob consumed my every thought. I wanted to tell this person how much he hurt my husband, but I was called to love him regardless of what he did to us.

Then, it hit me that if I say I love Jesus, I *must* obey His command to love others, which means, in this situation, to love this person because I love Christ. I knew I had to be patient with this person, could not take into account this wrong that we had suffered, and needed to endure all things. I knew that God alone would have to give me the strength to do this because, in my humanness, it wouldn't be easy.

The same would go for honoring a parent, a co-worker, a child, a spouse, or a friend with whom you are angry. Love them because Jesus calls you to. If we love Christ, we have to love others.

This fifth of the Ten Commandments is similar to the command of Jesus "Love your neighbor as yourself."

❖ Commandments 6-10: **Exodus 20:13-17: "You shall not murder. You shall not commit adultery. You shall not steal. You shall not give false testimony against your neighbor. You shall not covet your neighbor's house. You shall not covet your neighbor's wife, or his manservant or maidservant, his ox or donkey, or anything that belongs to your neighbor."**

Many people we know hate church because they feel it is only about a list of rules and regulations. "Do this" and "don't do that" are common themes in sermons today. What people do not realize is that these commands are for their own good. *What happens if you murder someone?* You will go to prison. *What happens if you commit adultery?* It will ruin your marriage and the lives of those around you. *What happens if you steal?* You might go to jail, get fired, or lose the trust of those around you. *What happens if you lie about someone?* Nobody will ever believe you again. *Why shouldn't you desire things that are not yours?* Doing so causes heartache and dissension.

Commandments 6-10 are about hurting other people. What is truly amazing is that what God commanded in the Old Testament, Jesus reinforced in the New Testament. How we love others and serve God demonstrates if our faith is real.

Matthew 22:37-40: "And He said to him, 'You shall love the Lord your God with all your heart, and with all your soul, and with all your mind.' This is the great and foremost commandment. The second is like it, 'You shall love your neighbor as yourself.' On these two commandments depend the whole Law and the Prophets."

All of this came together for me (Lisa) as I was trying to get over this situation that hurt Rob. I recognized for the first time that my claim to be a truly devoted follower of Jesus Christ would be tested in my response to this person. Did I truly love Jesus as I claimed? The Bible says that if I did, I would obey His commands, which meant I would have to love God first and this person second. I have to admit it was a struggle for many days.

As I started to pray each day for the strength to love this person, God provided it for me. Instead of waking up angry and tearful, I started waking up praying for this person and his walk with the Lord. I never really thought to pray much for him before, but now it seemed to be on my mind more and more. I wanted to love this person, and it all started with an act of obedience: recognizing I could not love him on my own. God ended up replacing my anger with His love.

Once we recognize that we cannot conjure up feelings of love, then we can finally do what God asks of us: surrender. Surrender our emotions and our feelings and let Him change us from the inside. The love I now feel is not something I made up; it is something God has placed in me. I did not want to be a part-time Christian and live a life in which I act one way when hurt and another way when things are going my way. I want to be a fully devoted follower of Jesus all of the time, and I recognized for the first time that love was the key to it all.

So, here is the test: do you love God above everything else and love others regardless of what they do to you? That is a true test of a fully devoted follower of Jesus Christ.

1 John 2:9-11: "The one who says he is in the Light and yet hates his brother is in the darkness until now. The one who loves his brother abides in the Light and there is no cause for stumbling in him. But the one who hates his brother is in the darkness and walks in the darkness, and does not know where he is going because the darkness has blinded his eyes."

John 14:15: "If you love Me, you will keep My commandments."

Chapter 7

FOLLOWERS OF JESUS DO NOT LIVE DOUBLE LIVES

A part-time Christian lives a double life. He has one foot in the world and the other in the church. But the Bible states clearly that to be a fully devoted follower of Jesus requires this:

1 John 2:15-17: "Do not love the world nor the things in the world. If anyone loves the world, the love of the Father is not in him. For all that is in the world, the lust of the flesh and the lust of the eyes and the boastful pride of life, is not from the Father, but is from the world. The world is passing away, and also its lusts; but the one who does the will of God lives forever."

As Christians, we are not to love the world. But what does that mean? How are we supposed to *not* love the world when we live *in* the world? How are we supposed to *not* love His creation, the ocean, the birds, and the stars? How are we supposed to *not* love our homes, our children, and our spouses who live in this world?

When the Bible uses the phrase "the world" here, it is referring to the world system. The world system cares for material possessions, money, lust, greed, and self more than anything else. Here are three things John said characterize a love of the world:

LUST OF THE FLESH

Psalm 78:18: "And in their heart they put God to the test by asking food according to their desire."

This verse refers to God providing manna for the children of Israel as they were wandering in the wilderness, but they were never satisfied. They wanted meat. They wanted what they did not have. Lust of the flesh could mean anything that we want that would go against God's best for us. Maybe a new spouse? Maybe a new job making more money but leaving less time to serve God? Maybe a new material possession? Maybe Alcohol? Drugs? Food? Shopping? The world system wants us to buy in to the lusts of the flesh, but God says we have to hate those things that will push us farther and farther away from Him.

Is making more money wrong? Is shopping or eating wrong? No, but when they become more important than our relationship with Christ, they become a lust of the flesh, which the Bible warns us against.

Romans 13:14: "But put on the Lord Jesus Christ, and make no provision for the flesh in regard to its lusts."

Titus 3:3: "For we also once were foolish ourselves, disobedient, deceived, enslaved to various lusts and pleasures, spending our life in malice and envy, hateful, hating one another."

1 Peter 2:11: "Beloved, I urge you as aliens and strangers to abstain from fleshly lusts which wage war against the soul."

Joshua 7:21: "When I saw among the spoil a beautiful mantle from Shinar and two hundred shekels of silver and a bar of gold fifty shekels in weight, then I coveted them and took them; and behold, they are concealed in the earth inside my tent with the silver underneath it."

Psalm 119:36: "Incline my heart to Your testimonies and not to dishonest gain."

LUST OF THE EYES

Another part of the world system comes from what we see that we want. Think of how much trouble we get into by looking at things we shouldn't look at. Think of the world of pornography and how addictions to it are ruining marriages and families daily. Why? The lust of the eyes. Satan has a great way to tempt us, and it doesn't take much more than a picture or advertisement. Maybe it is of a new car or television that we can't afford. Maybe it is the new secretary or the next door neighbor. Maybe it is a vacation home that we cannot afford. Lust of the eyes refers to anything that would take our focus off of serving the Lord.

The Bible says in **James 1:13-15, "Let no one say when he is tempted, 'I am being tempted by God'; for God cannot be tempted by evil, and He Himself does not tempt anyone. But each one is tempted when he is carried away and enticed by his own lust then when lust has conceived, it gives birth to sin; and when sin is accomplished, it brings forth death."**

Remember this: temptation is not sin, but when it becomes lust and the lust conceives, it becomes sin. The great thing is that God promises in **1 Corinthians 10:13** that **"No temptation has overtaken you but such as is common to man; and God is faithful, who will not allow you to be tempted beyond what you are able, but with the temptation will provide the way of escape also, so that you will be able to endure it."** God says that there is no temptation that has the power to overtake us; He always offers an escape. The question then becomes, will we take the escape or continue on a path of destruction?

Genesis 3:6: "When the woman saw that the tree was good for food, and that it was a delight to the eyes, and that the tree was desirable to make one wise, she took from its fruit and ate; and she gave also to her husband with her, and he ate."

Genesis 6:2: "That the sons of God saw that the daughters of men were beautiful; and they took wives for themselves, whomever they chose."

Job 31:1: "I have made a covenant with my eyes; how then could I gaze at a virgin?"

Psalm 119:37: "Turn away my eyes from looking at vanity, and revive me in Your ways."

Matthew 4:8: "Again, the devil took Him to a very high mountain and showed Him all the kingdoms of the world and their glory;"

BOASTFUL PRIDE OF LIFE

Pride is an ugly thing in the eyes of God. It tells God that *we* are in charge, *we* are in control, and everything is all about us. The world system wants us to buy in to that thought pattern. I John tells us that loving the world and the things of the world means our lives are devoted to ourselves. Do we recognize that all we have is from God? Our families, our homes, our jobs, and our friends are gifts from Him to be used for Him. The boastful pride of life says, "*I* earned this myself"; "*I* found my spouse on my own"; "My children will turn out great because of how *I* am raising them"; and "All my possessions are mine because of *my* hard work." Loving the world means we refuse to acknowledge that all we have is a gift from God. If we love the world, then we look to ourselves instead of looking to Him.

Daniel 4:30: "The king reflected and said, 'Is this not Babylon the great, which I myself have built as a royal residence by the might of my power and for the glory of my majesty?'"

As fully devoted followers of Jesus Christ, we recognize that the world system and God's system are two completely different entities. As followers of Christ, we recognize that our lives are not our own and that the lust of the flesh, the lust of the eyes, and the boastful pride of life are not options for us. On the other hand, a part-time Christian assumes that he can live in both worlds. However, the Bible clearly states that it is impossible to be a part of both worlds: if we love the world, we do not love God.

Are we being taught these principles in churches today? It is sad to us when we hear people say how they hate the "hell, fire and brimstone" messages that used to be preached many years ago. The problem is that many churches have gone the opposite way and go overboard in telling us that Jesus loves us and demands very little from us. But 1 John makes it clear that being fully devoted followers of Jesus Christ means that we do not have the option to love the world and its system; the Bible demands that we love and serve God more than anything else. It is time we get back to understanding that there is no room for part-time Christianity.

As fully devoted followers of Jesus Christ, we have to recognize that when we became Christians we all received a new job. We are now ambassadors: **"Therefore, we are ambassadors for Christ, as though God were making an appeal through us; we beg you on behalf of Christ, be reconciled to God" (2 Corinthians 5:20).** Think about what an ambassador is. The ambassador from China living in the United States is a foreigner. He represents his country back home. He cannot change his customs and behaviors just to fit into a different culture or he would lose his ability to be an ambassador. *The Greek-English Lexicon of the New Testament Based on Semantic Domains* says this of an ambassador:

* **To function as a representative of a ruling authority.** As Christians we represent Jesus as our ruling authority, and our lives are lived as His representatives. The world does not rule our lives; God's Word does.
* **Our work has been specially assigned by Christ.** An ambassador is assigned to his job and the same is true for us as Christians. We have been assigned to work for the Lord Jesus Christ in this world. This world is not our home, but heaven is and, therefore, our lives will reflect what He wants.[3]

2 Corinthians 5:20 makes it clear that we have the job of "recon-ciliation." Our lives should be lived with the purpose of reconciling people to God. All the people we come in contact with should see that we are not like the world. We represent the King of Kings, and our one desire is to share Him with those we come in contact with. That is our job as His representatives on this earth.

A fully devoted follower of Jesus Christ understands this concept, knows that time is short, and realizes that God put each of us in neighborhoods, families, and workplaces for the purpose of trying to reconcile others to Him. The world says life is about money, status, and prestige. But the Bible says it is about the people, all of whom need to have a personal relationship with God through Jesus. A part-time Christian has never recognized this call on his life. A part-time Christian is one who goes to work and lives at his home and in his neighborhood without any regard for what his true job is.

Which begs the question once again…

Is there such a thing, according to the Bible, as a part-time Christian?

Chapter 8

FOLLOWERS OF JESUS WILL PERSEVERE TO THE END

1 John 2:19: "They went out from us, but they were not really of us; for if they had been of us, they would have remained with us; but they went out, so that it would be shown that they all are not of us."

Here is an interesting thought that nobody wants to verbalize: if someone asks Jesus into his life, goes to church for awhile, and walks away from the church and his Christian life, the odds are pretty good the *he never was a Christian to begin with*. We can hear the groans already from those of you who think we are being judgmental. But look at what the Bible says: if they went out from us, they were not of us! That proclamation in the scripture makes the responses from people to this next question amazing. When we hear that someone has recently died, our first question usually is, "Was he or she a believer?" Here are some responses we often hear to that question:

- I think so.
- He went to church.
- She used to go to church.
- I don't think he was walking with the Lord.
- She believed in God.

- She was "sort of" a Christian.
- He was a very nice person.
- She was a great "family" person.
- He gave a lot of money to the church.

Responses like these make us want to ask the question again in a more precise way: "Was he or she a fully devoted follower of Jesus Christ?" See the difference? Anyone can be a nice, loving, giving person who believed in God and went to church, and believe it or not, this same person *may not be a Christian.* We have lost the sense of what it truly means to be a Christian, making us a confused group of people.

1 John tells us that if we walk away from our faith, we were never really His to begin with.

A fully devoted follower of Jesus Christ perseveres until the end. He is in a growth pattern, and his life should look different this year than it looked last year. Our greatest fear is the false sense of assurance that many churches are preaching: come to church, get baptized, and you are saved. That seems to often produce part-time Christian status. When a person's life has no reflection of a relationship with Christ, why would we assume he is saved?

If we are fully devoted followers of Jesus Christ, we would hope that our funeral service would be devoted to sharing Him with everyone present. We can understand that the answers above would be given if a person were a part-time Christian because part-time Christians are difficult to distinguish from non-Christians. Their lives never had an impact for Jesus on this world. Their lives were never lived in obedience to God's Word. They might have gone to church, but that was the extent of their Christian life.

Which begs the question once again...

Is there such a thing, according to the Bible, as a part-time Christian?

Take a look at these verses and see why the Bible says perseverance is key to our Christian lives.

1 Timothy 4:16: "Pay close attention to yourself and to your teaching; persevere in these things, for as you do this you will ensure salvation both for yourself and for those who hear you."

Luke 8:15: "But the seed in the good soil, these are the ones who have heard the word in an honest and good heart, and hold it fast, and bear fruit with perseverance."

Fully devoted followers of Jesus Christ pay attention to what they are taught. They persevere in all things–good or bad. They don't walk away from what they believe if something does not go their way. They press on, bearing fruit and holding fast.

Romans 2:7: "To those who by perseverance in doing good seek for glory and honor and immortality, eternal life."

2 Thessalonians 1:4: "Therefore, we ourselves speak proudly of you among the churches of God for your perseverance and faith in the midst of all your persecutions and afflictions which you endure."

1 Timothy 6:11: "But flee from these things, you man of God, and pursue righteousness, godliness, faith, love, perseverance and gentleness."

Revelation 1:9: "I, John, your brother and fellow partaker in the tribulation and kingdom and perseverance which are in Jesus, was on the island called Patmos because of the word of God and the testimony of Jesus."

Revelation 2:2" "I know your deeds and your toil and perseverance, and that you cannot tolerate evil men, and you put to the test those who call themselves apostles, and they are not, and you found them to be false."

Part of perseverance is making sure that what you are being taught is what the Bible truly says. Life is full of tribulation, toil, evil men, false teachers, and hypocrites. Perseverance means that you don't walk away from your faith when faced with any of those things. Truly devoted followers of Jesus Christ study God's Word, know the truth, and *cannot* walk away.

Revelation 2:19: "I know your deeds, and your love and faith and service and perseverance, and that your deeds of late are greater than at first."

Revelation 13:10: "If anyone is destined for captivity, to captivity he goes; if anyone kills with the sword, with the sword he must be killed. Here is the perseverance and the faith of the saints."

Revelation 14:12: "Here is the perseverance of the saints who keep the commandments of God and their faith in Jesus."

Even when faced with death or captivity, truly devoted followers of Jesus Christ will persevere to the end. They continue their love, service, and faith. We are always amazed to read stories about missionaries who persevered to the end under horrible circumstances and were martyred for their faith. Our hope and prayer is that under the same circumstances, we would respond in the same way.

This is how you can distinguish if someone is a part-time Christian: did he persevere to the end? 1 John makes it clear that a truly devoted follower of Jesus Christ keeps his faith until the end. His faith grows, at times slower than at others, but it grows nevertheless.

We are always amazed to go to funerals and hear how someone is in heaven because he accepted Jesus in his life when he was younger. Often, we know this person, know he never stepped foot into a church, never opened a Bible, and never once spoke of Jesus that we heard of, yet hundreds of people at the service just heard he is in heaven!

This madness has to stop! We are fooling people into thinking that part-time Christianity is normal. We are fooling people into thinking that heaven can be attained without a cost. Remember, salvation is a free gift, but once we are saved, our lives are no longer our own.

Our lives are now owned and controlled by the God of the universe. We are now His representatives on earth, we are His ambassadors, and we go where He tells us to go. We read His Word, we obey His commands, and our lives at work and home reflect Him. *That* is what a truly devoted follower of Jesus Christ is!

Is there such a thing, according to the Bible, as a part-time Christian?

Chapter 9

FOLLOWERS OF JESUS KNOW WHERE THEY WILL SPEND ETERNITY

1 John 5:11-13: "And the testimony is this, that God has given us eternal life, and this life is in His Son. He who has the Son has the life; he who does not have the Son of God does not have the life. These things I have written to you who believe in the name of the Son of God, so that you may know that you have eternal life."

A few years ago, we were invited to go to Italy with some friends of ours who are Catholic. They brought a friend of theirs along who was a priest, and each night for dinner, he sat with different people. One night, he sat with us which, of course, gave us a great opportunity to ask questions. As we were talking about the Catholic Church, we asked about his assurance of his salvation: did he know for sure that he would go to heaven when he died? He said that nobody ever could be sure of that. We were shocked and quickly quoted 1 John 5:11-13, explaining to him that God clearly wants us to *know* we have eternal life.

As dinner went on, we started asking questions about sin. We presented this scenario to him: if he were a priest all of his life, went out tonight and did something that was clearly sin, and then died tonight, would he go to heaven? He didn't think he would. As we talked, it became evident that this man was basing his salvation on his works; he believed that if he died with a sin in his life, he wouldn't make it to heaven. Doesn't that seem like a frightening way to live? Is that what the Bible says? Is it possible to give your life to God, do something wrong before you die, and then never make it to heaven?

The Bible must be the final authority in our lives, which means that whatever our church tells us or whatever traditions our church holds that contradict the Bible are false doctrines. These verses in 1 John 5 give us two truths that we can lay hold of and never let go of. Let's look at the first one:

"And the testimony is this, that God has given us eternal life, and this life is in His Son. He who has the Son has the life; he who does not have the Son of God does not have the life."

A part-time Christian is one who has not read the Bible enough to know that his salvation is completely secure. According to this verse, God has given us eternal life through His Son Jesus Christ. This verse makes it clear that salvation is not based on having good church attendance, doing really nice things for people, putting money in the offering plate on Sundays, or keeping all the Ten Commandments. The *only* thing that matters is if you have the Son.

That is a hard statement to accept in this day and age where we are taught that we have to work hard to make a living. The harder we work, the more benefits we have. Spiritually, the Bible gives us a different picture: it is not what we do for God that matters most; it is what He has done for us. The day we recognize that our sin has separated us from God and that we need Jesus in our lives to save us from the wrath of God is the day of our salvation. Once we have given our lives to Jesus–in the true biblical sense–we "have the Son."

The Bible says that once Jesus has taken up residence in our lives, we can be assured that we will spend eternity with Him. He is the reason we get to go to heaven. He is the reason we can have a relationship with God. He is the reason for everything in our lives. He who has the Son has the life; therefore, we can be assured of our salvation. We do not have to guess anymore about what will happen if we die. We can know for sure, without a doubt, that we will spend eternity in heaven with Him.

The second part of **1 John 5:13** gives us further assurance of our salvation: **"These things I have written to you who believe in the name of the Son of God, so that you may know that you have eternal life."** No more guessing. No more fearfulness. We can have true assurance because of something that Jesus did for us, not something we did for ourselves. Why do we believe this? Because the Bible tells us we can. Once again, we see the importance of reading His Word and learning these wonderful, comforting truths so that we have answers for those who are unsure of their eternal life.

Now, back to the question we asked the priest: can you lose your salvation if you do something wrong? Will you not go to heaven because you sin before you die? Let's look at the life of Peter, the big mouth disciple of Jesus. He was the headstrong fisherman who left everything to follow Jesus. Before Jesus was crucified, Jesus and Peter had the following conversation:

Matthew 26:33-35: "But Peter said to Him, 'Even though all may fall away because of You, I will never fall away.' Jesus said to him, 'Truly I say to you that this very night, before a rooster crows, you will deny Me three times.' Peter said to Him, 'Even if I have to die with You, I will not deny You.' All the disciples said the same thing too."

Here was Peter, confessing his undying loyalty to Jesus, yet Jesus knew him well enough to know that the fear of persecution and crucifixion would take its toll on Peter.

Matthew 26:69-75: "Now Peter was sitting outside in the court-yard, and a servant-girl came to him and said, 'You too were with Jesus the Galilean.' But he denied it before them all, saying, 'I do not know what you are talking about.' When he had gone out to the gateway, another servant-girl saw him and said to those who were there, 'This man was with Jesus of Nazareth.' And again he denied it with an oath, 'I do not know the man.' A

little later the bystanders came up and said to Peter, 'Surely you too are one of them; for even the way you talk gives you away.' Then he began to curse and swear, 'I do not know the man!' And immediately a rooster crowed. And Peter remembered the word which Jesus had said, 'Before a rooster crows, you will deny Me three times.' And he went out and wept bitterly."

Denying Jesus sounds like a death sentence to those who follow Him, for Peter must have remembered what Jesus said in **Luke 12:9: "but he who denies Me before men will be denied before the angels of God."** What a frightening time for Peter, who probably feared for his salvation now that he had denied Jesus. But here we see the difference between a part-time Christian and a fully devoted follower of Jesus Christ. Truly devoted followers recognize their sin, are remorseful over their sin, and turn from their sin. Peter did just those things. He didn't walk away from Jesus forever–he couldn't.

Peter also must have remembered this conversation with Jesus as he saw many who followed Him walk away from their faith. **John 6:66-69 says, "As a result of this many of His disciples withdrew and were not walking with Him anymore. So Jesus said to the twelve, 'You do not want to go away also, do you?' Simon Peter answered Him, 'Lord, to whom shall we go? You have words of eternal life. We have believed and have come to know that You are the Holy One of God.'"** Peter couldn't walk away from his faith because he recognized that Jesus alone has the words of eternal life. He recognized that Jesus is the "Holy One of God." This belief moved from his head to his heart and then to his feet as his denial was short lived. After the resurrection, Peter was a truly devoted follower of Jesus Christ until the day he was martyred by crucifixion.

So can you lose your salvation if you sin before you die and never have the chance to repent? If a person believed that, then he would be basing his salvation on what *he* did for God instead of what *Jesus* did for him. Do Christians sin? Absolutely. Does our sin that Jesus paid for on the cross ever return to us to deal with by ourselves? Absolutely not. Even though Peter sinned, he always recognized that his salvation was based on Jesus alone and not on himself.

The difference between Peter, who was a fully devoted follower of Jesus Christ, and a part-time Christian is that Peter dealt with his sin, never walked away from his faith, repented and followed Jesus to his death. A part-time Christian would sin, would expect God to forgive him because that is "just what God is supposed to do," and would not finish his faith to the end. Just like Judas who betrayed Jesus, a part-time Christian never finishes what he started.

How awesome Jesus is! Look what was said to Mary at the tomb after His resurrection:

Mark 16:5-18: "Entering the tomb, they saw a young man sitting at the right, wearing a white robe; and they were amazed. And he said to them, 'Do not be amazed; you are looking for Jesus the Nazarene, who has been crucified. He has risen; He is not here; behold, here is the place where they laid Him. But go, tell His disciples and Peter, "He is going ahead of you to Galilee; there you will see Him, just as He told you."'"

Peter had to feel awful about what he had done. He had to have felt confused, but in these verses the angel at Jesus' tomb specifically used Peter's name. He must have known how devastated Peter was at what he did, and the forgiveness offered to him is remarkable. Sometimes when we sin, we can get so down on ourselves and want to walk away from our faith because we feel that Jesus could never forgive us for what we have done. Yet here in this passage, it is clear that Jesus wanted Peter to know that he was forgiven. That is the Jesus that we as truly devoted followers have put our faith and trust in. That is why we can be confident that we will spend eternity in heaven with Him when we place our lives in His hands.

Chapter 10

FOLLOWERS OF JESUS UNDERSTAND PRAYER

1 John 5:14: "This is the confidence which we have before Him, that, if we ask anything according to His will, He hears us."

Have you ever wanted something so badly that you prayed for it constantly? Maybe you wanted a new boyfriend or girlfriend, so you prayed. Maybe your husband or wife was leaving you, so you prayed. Maybe you wanted a new job or a new school to attend, so you prayed. Maybe you had a wayward child, a financial crisis or a health problem, so you prayed.

What happened when your prayer was not answered the way you wanted? What happened when you never got that new job, you never got the boyfriend or girlfriend, and your wayward child ended up in prison? What happened when your spouse walked out the door and your friend still had cancer? Were you just slightly mad at God? Better yet, why do we continue to pray when we don't get the answers we ask for?

Most people have these tough questions, even though they may not voice them. Where were You, God? Why did You let this happen? Why didn't You stop it? Why didn't You heal her? Why did You allow me to get so hurt? And the questions go on, seemingly with no answers in sight. **1 John 5:14** gives us a clear answer: He hears us when we ask Him for things that line up with His plans for us.

For fully devoted followers of Jesus Christ, this verse makes total sense. We give our lives to Him to do whatever He wants with us. Once we understand that we are here for the purpose of loving Him, serving Him, and sharing Him with others, our prayer lives start to change. A part-time Christian, on the other hand, is here to serve himself. He goes to church and might attend a Bible study, but he never really grasps the truth about why he is here. Therefore, his prayers tend to be focused only on his personal goals, his personal life, his personal money, and his personal health.

Take a look at the differences between these two prayer lives:

A. God, please give me that job so I can make a lot of money.
B. God, please open the door for that job if that is the place I can best serve you and others.

A. God, please help that person to like me and want to date me.
B. God, please bring along the person that You have for me, someone who is completely devoted to You, so that we can serve You together.

A. God, all my life I wanted to attend that university. Please make sure I get in.
B. God, you know my heart's desire is to be at that university, but I am yours. I am here to serve you the best I can. I pray you will open the door to whatever university You want me to go to.

A. God, I need money to make my house payment–could you get me some?
B. God, you know how desperate I am this month, and You alone are the provider. You know how hard I have been working, but I cannot seem to get ahead. God, please open a door for me so that I can work overtime or do whatever I need to do so that I can pay these bills.

A. God, You know I want a child. That is all I have ever wanted, so please make sure I get pregnant.

B. God, You know all I have ever wanted in this life is to be a parent, but I know You alone are the giver of life, and You know what is best for me. If children are not in Your plans for me, then give me the ability to not be sad and to recognize that You have a different plan for my life.

A. God, please make my friend get better; please take away her sickness.

B. God, You are the Great Physician, and You can heal or not heal, depending on what You want to accomplish. Lord, I beg you to heal my friend, but if you do not, please use this sickness to bring others to You.

See the difference? One prayer life is centered on self, while the other prayer life is centered on God. Fully devoted followers of Jesus Christ recognize that we should want what God wants; anything other than His will for our lives will be disastrous. Part-time Christians do not understand that God wants what is best for us, which may be different than what we want for ourselves. Once we begin to believe what **Romans 8:28** says, then we can learn to trust in Him even when we don't get what we think we want: **"And we know that God causes all things to work together for good to those who love God, to those who are called according to His purpose."**

As truly devoted followers of Jesus Christ, our prayer lives are different because along with asking, we are trusting, which pleases God. We believe He wants us to ask Him for guidance, ask Him for what is on our hearts, and communicate with Him daily. However, within each request, we trust He will do what is best for our lives. Many times what God knows is best for us goes against our desires; that is where trusting Him comes in. We always tell our children as they are in the dating process, "If that person breaks up with you, that is God's protection over your life." Accepting that fact is so hard when emotions are involved, but if we can grasp the fact that God is protecting us, it should make the heartache hurt a little less.

We had a friend a few years ago who was going through a tremendous heartache. Through it all, we talked, we prayed, we cried, and then we prayed more. We begged God to turn the situation around, take the heartache away, and make it all better. But God decided to do something different, and years later we are *so* thankful that God did not answer our prayers in the way that we asked. If we are His children and are fully devoted followers of His, then we must learn to trust that He is in control of every circumstance in our lives.

Maybe your child who went to prison will find Jesus there. Maybe your spouse walked out the door because God was rescuing you from a life of heartache. Maybe by not having children of your own, God felt you would be a wonderful adoptive parent. Maybe that boyfriend who decided he didn't like you anymore was the wrong person for you in the long run. Maybe the sickness you have will allow for more opportunities to share Him with others.

See how this works? We don't have to worry anymore. We don't have to be mad at God if He doesn't answer our prayers in the way we want them answered. **Isaiah 55:9** says it best: **"For as the heavens are higher than the earth, so are My ways higher than your ways and My thoughts than your thoughts."** God doesn't think like we do, and His purposes are completely different from ours. All of the situations that He allows into our lives are to teach us something, help us grow in our faith, and move us to trust Him with everything.

Part-time Christians feel that God exists for one purpose: to serve *them*. They feel He should always give them what they want and always make sure they are happy and healthy. Unfortunately for many who adhere to this thinking, as the verse in 1 John says, He hears us when we ask for things that align with His will for our lives. Part-time Christians have never taken the time to learn that they are here on this earth, saved by the blood of Jesus, and called into a new life for one purpose: to serve Him with all their heart, soul, mind, and strength. In this life, what we ask Him for should be centered on our service to Him.

We also need to remember that prayer is a commandment. **1 Thessalonians 5:17** says, **"Pray without ceasing;..."** We are commanded to pray about everything because God wants to know that we trust Him with our day-to-day issues. Everything we pray about should center on the things that matter to Him. As fully devoted followers of Jesus Christ, we understand the importance of daily communication with the God of the universe who is ruler over our lives.

We cannot imagine *not* talking with Him about the important decisions in our lives like whom we should date, whom we should marry, and where we should work. We cannot imagine *not* talking to Him about those who are hurting or sick around us. As we pray for comfort and healing, we also know that if things don't turn out like we want, it is okay. We love Him and trust Him enough to know that His ways are best.

The next time one of your prayers is not answered the way you would like, instead of being mad, relax and give thanks! Know that the God to whom you entrusted your life has a greater plan, and His plan is always perfect. He just wants you to trust Him.

Chapter 11

FOLLOWERS OF JESUS HAVE
HAD A TRUE CONVERSION

As we are winding down this book, we want you to look at your own life and ask yourself these questions: Am I a part-time Christian? Do I care more for my life, my hobbies, my friends, and my family more than Jesus? Do I read my Bible daily so I can know Him better? Do I truly love those who are hard to love? Do I love the things of this world more than I love the things of God? Am I willing to do whatever it takes to persevere to the end? Do I live in a continual pattern of sin and refuse to repent? Are non-Christians often offended by my faith in Christ? Do I help those in need? Do I listen to what my pastor says with a heart to know if it is true? Do I study to find out if what I am being told is true? Am I sure I am going to heaven? Do I pray for the things *I* want or the things *God* wants in my life?

These are very hard questions, and depending on your answers, you may need to stop right now and ask yourself whether you are truly a Christian. The Bible is clear in **2 Corinthians 13:5**: **"Test yourselves to see if you are in the faith; examine yourselves! Or do you not recognize this about yourselves, that Jesus Christ is in you—unless indeed you fail the test?"** The questions above may be a shock to many readers. Maybe all of your life you just assumed you were a Christian because you go to church or even attend a Bible study. Maybe all your life you were taught that you just had to be a good person and put money in the offering plate in order to go to heaven. But maybe, for the first time, you are seeing what the *Bible* says it means to be a Christian.

Because many churches refuse to teach the hard truths of the Bible, many people assume they are spiritually sound. Many are being assured they are okay spiritually and assured that, because they do nice things, they are going to heaven. Our hope and prayer is that today will be the day you are confronted with the truth about what **true**, **biblical**, Christianity really is. Does the Bible say there is such a thing as a part-time Christian? Does the Bible say it is possible for a person to accept Jesus in his life and then have nothing change? Does the Bible say it is possible to go to church and Bible study yet live the remaining hours each week for yourself?

The Bible calls us to be truly devoted followers of Jesus Christ. Yes, we still sin. Yes, we still stumble. Yes, we still say and do stupid and ungodly things. But the difference is that the Holy Spirit living within us will not let those things go unaddressed. It is His job to convict us, change us, and give us the power to walk away from sinful lifestyles. It is His job to transform our lives from the inside, and because of His transforming work, we will look more and more like Jesus each day.

Truly devoted followers of Jesus Christ are in His Word on a daily basis, desiring to know Him and His will for our lives. We try desperately to love those who are hard to love, knowing that doing that takes obedience over emotion. We hate the world system. We dislike hearing the Lord's name used in vain. We despise the things we see on TV that do not align with the heart of God. We know the Christian life is hard to live, yet we also know we are in this until the end. We cannot live in continual patterns of sin because the Holy Spirit refuses to leave us alone until we repent. We are not hurt when our unbelieving friends and family don't want to be around us because we understand that the darkness hates the light. We desire to know the truths of God so we will never be swept away by false teaching. We take God at His word that we will spend eternity with Him, and we recognize that prayer not answered our way is a blessing from God in the long run.

So, we ask again—which one are you? If your life does not look like the life we just described, we beg you to surrender your life to Jesus, give everything over to Him, and let Him change your life. Start reading your Bible consistently, not just to say you read it but to let His Word change your life. Start acting on what you are being taught. Give your life away to others. Obey His commandments. Our desperate hope and prayer for this book is that you would experience a true conversion today. A true conversion is one that starts you on this journey of being a fully devoted follower of Jesus Christ. It doesn't happen in a day or a month; it happens over a lifetime!

As you begin your new life in Christ, your life will become more and more about Jesus and less and less about yourself. Your hobbies and your work will take on new meaning. How you treat your spouse and children will take on new meaning. The changes happen slowly, but they are guaranteed to happen. **Philippians 1:6** makes it clear that you will change: **"For I am confident of this very thing, that He who began a good work in you will perfect it until the day of Christ Jesus."** Paul added to this thought in **2 Corinthians 5:17:** **"Therefore if anyone is in Christ, he is a new creature; the old things passed away; behold, new things have come."** If you have made the decision to surrender your life to Christ, recognize this: you are a new creature. Your old life has passed away.

Remember the polar bear analogy in the preface? Remember the nature they are born with? The Bible says in **John 3:3, "Jesus answered and said to him, 'Truly, truly, I say to you, unless one is born again he cannot see the kingdom of God.'"** Just like the bear who is born with a nature to hunt and swim in cold water, you as a "born again" Christian also have a nature—a new one. It is a nature that wants to please God, wants to grow closer to Him, and wants to help others. It is a nature that refuses to allow you to continue in sin and refuses to allow you to be hateful and unforgiving. It is a nature that desires the things of God over the things of the world.

Think of a world made up of truly devoted followers of Jesus Christ. Think of what our neighborhoods, our sports teams, and our workplaces would be like. There would be no more lying, cheating, and giving someone our word only to disregard what was said. There would be no more adultery, sex before marriage, and homosexuality among those claiming to be Christians. No more would we hear people say to us, "But I thought he was a Christian." Instead, we would see people living out their faith. If they sin, they repent. If they hurt someone, they apologize. If they see someone hurting, they help them.

This world will never be impacted for Jesus with part-time Christians running around. This book is a call to all of those who live their lives completely differently during the week than they do on Sunday. This book is a call to those who refuse to take God and His Word seriously. This book is a call to those who think they are Christians just because they go to church or a Bible Study. True Christians—truly devoted followers of Jesus Christ—are impacted by Jesus daily: at work, at home, at dance, or at soccer. We are Christians because God has called us to Himself and saved us so we could serve Him. Our hope and prayer is that if you fall under the part-time Christian category, you will stop, recognize the problem, and move to the fully devoted follower of Jesus Christ category today.

Surrender your life today, recognizing that the Bible tells us we *will* be different if we are His. No longer can we do the things we did before because, remember, we have a new nature. No longer do we *want* to do the things we did before because, as we read His Word, the Holy Spirit uses it to change us. No longer are we content doing the Christian thing on a part-time basis. Now, it affects every area of our lives.

That is what happens when you become a fully devoted follower of Jesus Christ!

Our hope and prayer is that you see what the *Bible* says a true Christian is. A true Christian reads his Bible to gain knowledge and acts on what he reads. A true Christian loves those who are hard to love. A true Christian helps those in need. A true Christian makes sure what he is hearing is the truth and is not swayed by false teaching. A true Christian understands prayers that are answered differently than what he asked for. A true Christian hates the things the world offers, knows others will not like him when he takes a stand for his faith, and knows where he is going when he dies.

So the question remains...

Are you a fully devoted follower of Jesus Christ?

Chapter 12

FOLLOWERS OF JESUS LIVE
OUT SCRIPTURE

To conclude this book, we wanted to provide for you some verses in the Bible that shows how a fully devoted follower of Jesus Christ is supposed to live. With so many verses to read at one time, the tendency is for readers to skip over this chapter or just skim over the verses. *We beg you not to do this*. This chapter is the most important in this book. God's Word, which is the final authority in our lives, can show us what our lives must look if we are to be His followers. Please read through these verses slowly and surrender your will to Him, allowing Him to change those things in your life that need to be changed.. Living these verses out will not only affect you and your family but it will also have an enormous impact for Jesus on everyone you meet. Living these verses out, you will prove to others that you really are a truly devoted follower of Jesus Christ!

FOLLOWERS OF JESUS ARE NOT SWAYED BY FALSE DOCTRINE.

Ephesians 4:14: "As a result, we are no longer to be children, tossed here and there by waves and carried about by every wind of doctrine, by the trickery of men, by craftiness in deceitful scheming."

FOLLOWERS OF JESUS SPEAK TRUTH.

Ephesians 4:25: "Therefore, laying aside falsehood, speak truth each one of you with his neighbor, for we are members of one another."

FOLLOWERS OF JESUS UNDERSTAND ANGER.

Ephesians 4:26-27: "Be angry, and yet do not sin; do not let the sun go down on your anger, and do not give the devil an opportunity."

FOLLOWERS OF JESUS DO NOT STEAL.

Ephesians 4:28: "He who steals must steal no longer; but rather he must labor, performing with his own hands what is good, so that he will have something to share with one who has need."

FOLLOWERS OF JESUS WATCH HOW THEY TALK.

Ephesians 4:29: "Let no unwholesome word proceed from your mouth, but only such a word as is good for edification according to the need of the moment, so that it will give grace to those who hear."

Ephesians 5:4: "And there must be no filthiness and silly talk, or coarse jesting, which are not fitting, but rather giving of thanks."

FOLLOWERS OF JESUS PUT AWAY BITTERNESS AND ANGER.

Ephesians 4:31: "Let all bitterness and wrath and anger and clamor and slander be put away from you, along with all malice."

FOLLOWERS OF JESUS ARE KIND AND FORGIVING.

Ephesians 4:32: "Be kind to one another, tender-hearted, forgiving each other, just as God in Christ also has forgiven you."

FOLLOWERS OF JESUS IMITATE GOD.

Ephesians 5:1: "Therefore be imitators of God, as beloved children."

FOLLOWERS OF JESUS ARE NOT IMMORAL.

Ephesians 5:3: "But immorality or any impurity or greed must not even be named among you, as is proper among saints."

FOLLOWERS OF JESUS UNDERSTAND THAT THEIR LIFESTYLE IS IMPORTANT.

Ephesians 5:5: "For this you know with certainty, that no immoral or impure person or covetous man, who is an idolater, has an inheritance in the kingdom of Christ and God."

FOLLOWERS OF JESUS DO NOT PARTICIPATE IN UNFRUITFUL DEEDS.

Ephesians 5:11: "Do not participate in the unfruitful deeds of darkness, but instead even expose them."

FOLLOWERS OF JESUS MAKE THE MOST OF THEIR TIME.

Ephesians 5:15-16: "Therefore be careful how you walk, not as unwise men but as wise, making the most of your time, because the days are evil."

FOLLOWERS OF JESUS ARE FILLED WITH THE SPIRIT.

Ephesians 5:18: "And do not get drunk with wine, for that is dissipation, but be filled with the Spirit."

FOLLOWERS OF JESUS UNDERSTAND HIS CALL
FOR WIVES.

Ephesians 5:22: "Wives, be subject to your own husbands, as to the Lord."

FOLLOWERS OF JESUS UNDERSTAND HIS CALL
FOR HUSBANDS.

Ephesians 5:25: "Husbands, love your wives, just as Christ also loved the church and gave Himself up for her."

FOLLOWERS OF JESUS UNDERSTAND HIS CALL
FOR CHILDREN.

Ephesians 6:1: "Children, obey your parents in the Lord, for this is right."

FOLLOWERS OF JESUS DO NOT PROVOKE
THEIR CHILDREN.

Ephesians 6:4: "Fathers, do not provoke your children to anger, but bring them up in the discipline and instruction of the Lord."

FOLLOWERS OF JESUS WORK HARD FOR
THEIR EMPLOYERS.

Ephesians 6:5-8: "Slaves, be obedient to those who are your masters according to the flesh, with fear and trembling, in the sincerity of your heart, as to Christ; not by way of eyeservice, as men-pleasers, but as slaves of Christ, doing the will of God from

the heart. With good will render service, as to the Lord, and not to men, knowing that whatever good thing each one does, this he will receive back from the Lord, whether slave or free."

FOLLOWERS OF JESUS TREAT THEIR EMPLOYEES WITH RESPECT.

Ephesians 6:9: "And masters, do the same things to them, and give up threatening, knowing that both their Master and yours is in heaven, and there is no partiality with Him."

FOLLOWERS OF JESUS SHARE HIM WITH OTHERS.

Galatians 1:15-16: "But when God, who had set me apart even from my mother's womb and called me through His grace, was pleased to reveal His Son in me so that I might preach Him among the Gentiles, I did not immediately consult with flesh and blood."

FOLLOWERS OF JESUS DO NOT CARRY OUT THE DESIRES OF THEIR FLESH.

Galatians 5:16-17: "But I say, walk by the Spirit, and you will not carry out the desire of the flesh. For the flesh sets its desire against the Spirit, and the Spirit against the flesh; for these are in opposition to one another, so that you may not do the things that you please."

FOLLOWERS OF JESUS RECOGNIZE FLESHLY DEEDS AND REFUSE TO OBEY THE LUSTS OF THE FLESH.

Galatians 5:19-21: "Now the deeds of the flesh are evident, which are: immorality, impurity, sensuality, idolatry, sorcery, enmities, strife, jealousy, outbursts of anger, disputes, dissensions, factions, envying, drunkenness, carousing, and things like these, of which I forewarn you, just as I have forewarned you, that those who practice such things will not inherit the kingdom of God."

FOLLOWERS OF JESUS BEAR THE FRUIT OF THE SPIRIT.

Galatians 5:22-24: "But the fruit of the Spirit is love, joy, peace, patience, kindness, goodness, faithfulness, gentleness, self-control; against such things there is no law. Now those who belong to Christ Jesus have crucified the flesh with its passions and desires."

FOLLOWERS OF JESUS WALK IN THE SPIRIT DAILY.

Galatians 5:25: "If we live by the Spirit, let us also walk by the Spirit."

FOLLOWERS OF JESUS DO NOT ENVY.

Galatians 5:26: "Let us not become boastful, challenging one another, envying one another."

FOLLOWERS OF JESUS UNDERSTAND THAT THEIR LIVES ARE TO BE LIVED FOR HIM.

Philippians 1:21-24: "For to me, to live is Christ and to die is gain. But if I am to live on in the flesh, this will mean fruitful labor for me; and I do not know which to choose. But I am hard-pressed from both directions, having the desire to depart and be with Christ, for that is very much better; yet to remain on in the flesh is more necessary for your sake."

FOLLOWERS OF JESUS CONDUCT THEMSELVES AS PEOPLE WORTHY OF THE GOSPEL.

Ephesians 4:1-2: "Therefore I, the prisoner of the Lord, implore you to walk in a manner worthy of the calling with which you have been called, with all humility and gentleness, with patience, showing tolerance for one another in love."

Philippians 1:27: "Only conduct yourselves in a manner worthy of the gospel of Christ, so that whether I come and see you or remain absent, I will hear of you that you are standing firm in one spirit, with one mind striving together for the faith of the gospel;"

FOLLOWERS OF JESUS UNDERSTAND THAT THEY WILL SUFFER FOR THEIR FAITH.

Philippians 1:29: "For to you it has been granted for Christ's sake, not only to believe in Him, but also to suffer for His sake."

FOLLOWERS OF JESUS DO NOT GRUMBLE OR ARGUE.

Philippians 2:14-15: "Do all things without grumbling or disputing; so that you will prove yourselves to be blameless and innocent, children of God above reproach in the midst of a crooked and perverse generation, among whom you appear as lights in the world."

FOLLOWERS OF JESUS COUNT ALL THINGS AS LOSS FOR THE SAKE OF CHRIST.

Philippians 3:7-8: "But whatever things were gain to me, those things I have counted as loss for the sake of Christ. More than that, I count all things to be loss in view of the surpassing value of knowing Christ Jesus my Lord, for whom I have suffered the loss of all things, and count them but rubbish so that I may gain Christ."

FOLLOWERS OF JESUS FORGET THE PAST AND LOOK TO THE FUTURE.

Philippians 3:12-14: "Not that I have already obtained it or have already become perfect, but I press on so that I may lay hold of that for which also I was laid hold of by Christ Jesus. Brethren, I do not regard myself as having laid hold of it yet; but one thing I do: forgetting what lies behind and reaching forward to what lies ahead, I press on toward the goal for the prize of the upward call of God in Christ Jesus."

FOLLOWERS OF JESUS DWELL ON THE RIGHT THINGS.

Philippians 4:8: "Finally, brethren, whatever is true, whatever is honorable, whatever is right, whatever is pure, whatever is lovely, whatever is of good repute, if there is any excellence and if anything worthy of praise, dwell on these things."

FOLLOWERS OF JESUS CONSIDER IT JOY WHEN THEY ENCOUNTER TRIALS.

James 1:2-4: "Consider it all joy, my brethren, when you encounter various trials, knowing that the testing of your faith produces endurance. And let endurance have its perfect result, so that you may be perfect and complete, lacking in nothing."

FOLLOWERS OF JESUS PERSEVERE UNDER TRIAL.

James 1:12: "Blessed is a man who perseveres under trial; for once he has been approved, he will receive the crown of life which the Lord has promised to those who love Him."

FOLLOWERS OF JESUS MUST BE QUICK TO HEAR, SLOW TO SPEAK, AND SLOW TO BECOME ANGRY.

James 1:19-20: "This you know, my beloved brethren. But everyone must be quick to hear, slow to speak and slow to

anger; for the anger of man does not achieve the righteousness of God."

FOLLOWERS OF JESUS MUST BE DOERS OF THE WORD.

James 1:22: "But prove yourselves doers of the word, and not merely hearers who delude themselves."

FOLLOWERS OF JESUS CARE FOR OTHERS.

James 1:27: "Pure and undefiled religion in the sight of our God and Father is this: to visit orphans and widows in their distress, and to keep oneself unstained by the world."

FOLLOWERS SHOW THEIR FAITH BY THEIR WORKS.

James 2:14-17: "What use is it, my brethren, if someone says he has faith but he has no works? Can that faith save him? If a brother or sister is without clothing and in need of daily food, and one of you says to them, 'Go in peace, be warmed and be filled,' and yet you do not give them what is necessary for their body, what use is that? Even so faith, if it has no works, is dead, being by itself."

FOLLOWERS OF JESUS UNDERSTAND WHAT WISDOM LOOKS LIKE.

James 3:17: "But the wisdom from above is first pure, then peaceable, gentle, reasonable, full of mercy and good fruits, unwavering, without hypocrisy."

FOLLOWERS OF JESUS ASK FOR THINGS WITH RIGHT MOTIVES.

James 4:3: "You ask and do not receive, because you ask with wrong motives, so that you may spend it on your pleasures."

FOLLOWERS OF JESUS SUBMIT TO GOD.

James 4:7-8a: "Submit therefore to God. Resist the devil and he will flee from you. Draw near to God and He will draw near to you."

Our hope and prayer as we end this book is that if you have found yourself to be a part-time Christian, you will turn your life over to Jesus today and start a new life as a truly devoted follower of Jesus Christ. Our prayer is that you will read your Bible and ask God daily to change your life so you will look more and more like a true Christian who will impact this world for Jesus! Our greatest fear is for those who can live a continual, part time Christian life without ever realizing that their eternal destiny could be at stake. This is a serious issue. Please examine your own life and make sure you find yourself in the "fully devoted follower of Jesus Christ" category which is the one and only road to eternal life in heaven!

If you have any questions or comments, please contact us at www.dollarchristianbooks.com.

We could not end this book without thanking our pastors and elders at West Valley Bible Church for the incredibly strong biblical teaching that comes from the pulpit each week. We are grateful for their hearts for the lost, the poor, and the hurting. We are also grateful for all the men and women in our small group who teach us and pray for us in times of trouble. You have made such an impact on our lives.

We also could not end this book without acknowledging the Mash Unit in Casa Grande. Jerry, you and your team are the most amazing people we know. Your love for Jesus and for

hurting people is such a testimony to us. We appreciate the time and effort you and Clarence devote to bringing food to Surprise, Arizona, so that we can mirror the Manna program. The endless hours you both put in to serve our Lord inspire us all. Thank you for the hard work you do. You are true examples of "fully devoted followers of Jesus Christ".

Rob and Lisa

Endnotes

1 Nicky Cruz, *Soul Obsession* (Colorado Springs, CO: Waterbook Press, 2005), 62-63.

2 Source material for this paragraph includes: Personal interview with Brad Melton (www.BradMelton.org); Moses 1:1-4 and Abraham 3:22-28 in *The Pearl of Great Price*; "Jesus Christ, Our Chosen Leader" in *Gospel Principles* (Salt Lake City, UT: LDS Church, 1997); "After All We Can Do" in *Becoming Gods* by Richard Abanes (Eugene, OR: Harvest House, 2004).

3 Johannes P. Louw, Ed. *The Greek-English Lexicon of the New Testament Based on Semantic Domains* (England: United Bible Societies, 1988).